"Poetry is the expression of the heart and mind of a pers
reflects on the person and work of Jesus, the expression is hopeful and redemptive. As an artist who uses words as expression, I found joy in reading *My Heart Cries Out*. This work connects with the human condition in a unique and awesome way."

Lecrae, hip-hop recording artist

"For some years now, Paul Tripp has delivered soul-reaching wisdom and timeless encouragement centered around the gospel and grace of Jesus, from which I have greatly benefited. It doesn't take much reading of Tripp's work to recognize that under his skin there is an artist lurking. In this collection of meditations, he artfully paints pictures that resonate deep in our souls as he walks with us through the pain and struggles of this world while also helping us see the glory of God's grace."

TobyMac, hip-hop recording artist; music producer; songwriter

"As with a timeless hymn lyric, Tripp has the great ability to grasp the vast riches of biblical truth and distill it for us in creative, compelling, and wonderfully practical ways. His writing has regularly shaped how we think as individuals, parents, and songwriters."

Keith and Kristyn Getty, hymn writers; recording artists

"One of Paul Tripp's great gifts to us is his ability to communicate profound truths in ways that are not only clear and searching, but also beautiful. With this collection of poems and meditations, he leans in to that gift to give us something that is, on the one hand, completely new, and on the other, familiar in its wisdom, insight, and honesty."

Russ Ramsey, Pastor, Christ Presbyterian Church, Nashville, Tennessee; author, Retelling the Story series

"As I read these meditations, I couldn't help but wonder if they are the types of prayers the Holy Spirit speaks on our behalf when our groans are too deep for words. *My Heart Cries Out* is a beautiful, honest, and grace-filled collection of reflections from a heart that has been near to the Lord for many years. Your heart will cry out indeed—cry out for joy and thanksgiving as you read the pages of this wonderful book."

Trillia Newbell, author, *Sacred Endurance*; *If God Is for Us*; and *God's Very Good Idea*

"So often these days, Christianity is presented solely as an intellectual enterprise, a faith that speaks only to the mind. But the Christian faith is so much more. God wants more than your thought life; he wants your emotional life too. He wants and demands all of your life. That is why Paul Tripp's *My Heart Cries Out* is such a needed project for today. Not only are the words in this book beautiful, they are beautifully honest. In *My Heart Cries Out*, Tripp will help you think, feel, and live out your love for God."

Thomas J. Terry, Executive Director, Humble Beast; member, Beautiful Eulogy; Lead Pastor, Trinity Church of Portland

"As a sage with scars, Paul Tripp offers us contemplation, transparency, beauty, and verse spoken straight from his soul. But the impact of this book surfaces not in the scope of Tripp's gifts or weakness but in the page-by-page celebration of God's unrelenting grace. If you're looking for a daily, creative, and soul-nourishing drip of gospel truth, feast upon the pages of this book!"

Dave Harvey, Teaching Pastor, Summit Church, Fort Myers, Florida; author, *When Sinners Say "I Do"* and *Letting Go*

"Art and poetry allow truth to enter the mind through the imagination where intellect often builds a wall of resistance. In this relatable anthology, Paul Tripp explores the tension between the 'already' and the 'not yet' in such a way that comforts the conscience and highlights the sweetness of God's forgiveness. In each meditation, you will find yourself. In each meditation, you will find Christ."

Flame, Grammy-nominated recording artist

"This book is theologically rich, biblically faithful, and devotionally nourishing for the soul. My heart was stirred, and my love for the Savior inflamed! Read and be blessed. Read and worship."

Daniel L. Akin, President, Southeastern Baptist Theological Seminary

My Heart Cries Out

Gospel Meditations for Everyday Life

PAUL DAVID TRIPP

 CROSSWAY®

WHEATON, ILLINOIS

TO JESUS

You have done what nothing or no one has been able to do.

You have turned my life into verse

and my journey into song.

Contents

Preface

I am not a poet; I am a pilgrim.

I am not attracted to formal, overly romantic Christian verse, but I think that we do not train our eyes to see enough, our hearts to consider enough, and our emotions to celebrate enough the glories of the grace that is showered down on us in a thousand ways every day. What you are about to read are notes from my journey through the struggle of God's amazing grace. These are my meditations on the intersection between God's ever-present grace and my ever-present battle to live out of the resources of that grace while I walk my way through this sadly broken and dysfunctional world.

You may be wondering why I used both the words "glories" and "struggle" to describe a life of grace. Well, God's grace is glorious. It is the single stellar glory of the life of God's children. There is no glory in this created world, no matter how beautiful, that can compete with the beauty of God's rescuing, forgiving, transforming, empowering, and delivering grace. There is no human achievement, no personal accomplishment, and no community victory that can do for us what God's grace can do. There is nothing that we can be given that can accomplish in us and for us what God's grace can. There is no other love that has the power to do what the amazing grace of God's boundless love can do for us. This grace really is so counterintuitive and mind-blowing that we will spend all of eternity performing exegesis on it, celebrating it, and worshiping the giver for it.

Yet, between the "already" of our conversion and the "not yet" of our home-going, God's grace doesn't always look like grace. Instinctively we think that God's grace will be a warm hug, a cool drink, an encouraging word, or a motivating insight. We look for grace to relieve and release us, and sometimes it does, but God's grace regularly comes to us in uncomfortable forms. God's grace causes us to face things in ourselves that are hard to see, consider, accept, and confess. Often God's grace takes us into things we would like to avoid, things that are hard, discouraging, and sad. God's grace will not only give us wonderful gifts, but it will also take precious things away from us. It will not only tell us the best news ever, it will also force us to accept the worst news we could ever be told. It will not only tell us that God is strong, but it will remind us of how weak we are without him. It will not only gift us with incredible wisdom, it will require us to face the fact that sin reduces all of us to fools. God's grace will not only introduce us to the only one in the entire universe who is truly worthy of our worship, but will also expose the catalog of God's replacements that regularly capture the affections of our hearts.

One of the primary struggles of the Christian life is this: grace doesn't always seem attractive to us. You see, there is often a difference between what we think we need and what our God of grace knows we need. And even if we are right in knowing what we need, we fail to understand what is necessary to produce that needed thing in us. So often we'd rather have a season when life is easy, predictable, and the people around us are drama-free than a season where transforming grace takes us to new depths of humility, understanding, maturity, and worship. So in each of our lives grace is both a glory and a struggle.

What you are about to read are my honest meditations on that struggle. They are my spontaneous responses to my journey through glory and struggle. They are:

celebratory hymns

disappointing cries

pleas for help

groans of confusion

shouts of joy

theological meditations

desperate requests

heartfelt confessions

hope for help in temptation

quiet contemplations

honest notes along the journey

They were not written as I sat looking out the window
of my country cottage (I don't have one of those) over a
pastoral scene on a poet's retreat. They were written:

early in the morning

late at night

in physical suffering

waiting for tea at Starbucks

on the plane

in the car

in the middle of a meal

when my heart was broken

when my heart was filled with joy

when I was at the end of my rope

when what was around me was hard

when what I saw in me caused grief

when God seemed distant

when I saw my sin clearly

when I basked in God's forgiveness

when weakness seemed in me and all around me

when I knew God was near

when resting in grace was a struggle

when I knew I'd have strength for the battle

when grace seemed glorious after all

These meditations have been generating and marinating for years. They are the transparent interactions of one man with the Savior of grace. My hope is that this volume will help you to see the Savior more clearly, to understand his grace more deeply, to confess your struggle more honestly, to worship him more fully, and to find in these meditations the motivation to continue to follow the Savior even when he's leading you into unexpected and hard places. My prayer is that these meditations will stimulate a worship, rest, and celebration in you that the difficulties of life, this side of eternity, will not have the power to end.

My Heart Cries Out

My heart cries out,
but I am not
afraid,
discouraged,
panicked,
forgotten,
alone,
dismayed,
or doubtful
because in the din
of a million voices
from every place,
in every situation,
young and old
crying day and night
in weakness,
in alienation,
in fear,
and in distress,
you are not
overwhelmed,
you are not
distracted,
you are not
disgusted,
you are not
discouraged,
you are not
exhausted.
But you listen,
you hear,
you attend to
my cry
in tenderness of
mercy,
in patience of
spirit,
and with generosity of
love.
You listen to my
plea
and you never
turn
away.
But with power and wisdom
and the tender heart of a
Savior,
you do this amazing thing—
you answer.

————

For the eyes of the Lord are on the
    righteous,
      and his ears are open to their
      prayer. (1 Pet. 3:12)

When do you cry out to the Lord?

Do you ever slip into thinking that
the Lord might be "overwhelmed,"
"distracted," "discouraged," or
"exhausted" by your situation?

For further study and encouragement,
read Genesis 16.

Hope

The only hope,
the only help,
the only rescue,
the only healing,
the only solace,
the only balm,
the only redemption,
the only restoration
for a broken,
dysfunctional,
sin-scarred,
evil-infected,
morally fallen,
dark, and dangerous
world
isn't found in
information,
socialization,
education,
political solution,
psychological insight,
or personal reformation,
but in the willing
birth,
righteousness,
humiliation,
suffering,
sacrifice,
and resurrection
of a God-man Redeemer.
No idea can liberate,
no power can save,
no institution can redeem,
restore,
resuscitate,
or recreate
what sin has destroyed.
So a Son had to come.
Son of God.
Son of Man.
The Creator
came to recreate.
The Savior came to be
the sacrifice.
The blessed one
came to suffer,
and in suffering
to bless the world with hope,
help,
rescue,
healing,
solace,
balm,
redemption,
and restoration.
The cost of it all was
his life.
It was his birth mission,
his resurrection victory.
History marched toward his coming;
there was no other way.

———

May the God of hope fill you with all joy and peace in believing,
so that by the power of the Holy Spirit you may abound in hope.
(Rom. 15:13)

What common things do you turn to as a source of hope? How do these things fall short when compared to the hope Christ offers you?

Meditate on and journal about the ways Christ has brought you hope.

For further study and encouragement, read 1 Corinthians 15.

First

It's not first about my
religious acts,
my spiritual duty, or the
degree of my obedience.
It's not first about what
I believe,
the precision of my theology,
or the truthfulness of the creed
I embrace.
It's not first about what
I give,
the regularity of my charity,
or the amount of my benevolence.
It's not first about
my teaching, my preaching,
or the truths I have shared with
     others.
It's not first about
my humility, my faithfulness,
or the extent of my obedience.
It's first about you—
your righteousness,
your wisdom,
your power,
your authority,
your grace—and how
you have unleashed all of them for
my forgiveness,
my rescue,
my redemption.
My life is no longer about
me;
it is first and foremost about
you.

———

For by grace you have been saved
through faith. And this is not your
own doing; it is the gift of God, not
a result of works, so that no one may
boast. (Eph. 2:8–9)

What elements of your spiritual and
religious life are you most likely to
pride yourself in?

How can you go about today making
sure that Jesus is first in your life?

For further study and encouragement,
read John 13:1–20.

But I Can't

I wish I could commend
my righteousness to you,
but I can't.
I wish I could brag of
my strength to you,
but I can't.
I wish I could boast about my wisdom
    to you,
but I can't.
I wish I could point you to my track
    record,
but I can't.
I wish I could tell you that I have no
    regrets,
but I can't.
You know me better than
I know myself.
I never escape your eye.
You search the deepest

regions of my heart.
You know my thoughts before
they are conscious to me.
You know my words before
I hear myself speak them.
You examine my desires before
they move me to action.
So without pretense or inadequate
    excuse,
stripped of pride and self-defense,
I bow before you,
devoid of demand or argument,
and I make one plea.
It is for your mercy.
I have come to accept
what you know of me,
and I cry for one thing—
grace.

———

For thus says the One who is high and lifted up,
  who inhabits eternity, whose name is Holy:
"I dwell in the high and holy place,
  and also with him who is of a contrite and lowly spirit,
to revive the spirit of the lowly,
and to revive the heart of the contrite." (Isa. 57:15)

Pray and search through your heart—are there sins you excuse or defend, is there pride or pretense, or do you demand something from God because of your self-righteousness? Humbly offer your discoveries to God.

Review your knowledge of various biblical heroes, particularly considering the moments when God revealed sin in their hearts. How did they react? (To help get started, see Job 38–42:6 or 2 Samuel 12.)

For further study and encouragement, read Psalm 139.

But Never

You humble me,
but never humiliate me.
You confront me,
but never mock me.
You warn me,
but never abandon me.
You call me,
but never leave me alone.
You discipline me,
but never beat me up.
You command me,
but never fail to enable me.
You see into my heart,
but never reject me for what you see.
You teach me your mysteries,
but never make fun of how much I don't know.
You stay near to me,
but you never tire of me.
You place your love on me,
but never withdraw it when I fail.
So I love you,
but I have come to understand that
my hope and security,
my present and my future,
my acceptance and identity,
my ability and potential,
are not in my love for you,
but in your shocking,
unfailing,
faithful,
wise,
and powerful
love for me.

———

Who shall separate us from the love of Christ?
Shall tribulation, or distress, or persecution, or
famine, or nakedness, or danger, or sword? As it
is written,

> *"For your sake we are being killed all the day*
> *long;*
> *we are regarded as sheep to be*
> *slaughtered."*

No, in all these things we are more than conquerors
through him who loved us. (Rom. 8:35–37)

Recall as many times as you can where God
promises to "never" do something in Scripture.

Do you fully base all of your life in God's love
for you?

For further study and encouragement, read
Ephesians 2.

Hard Moments

Hard moments
between the already and the not yet.
Hard moments
in a world gone bad.
Hard moments
when temptation seduces.
Hard moments
with body weak and mind tired.
Hard moments
when friends promise, but betray.
Hard moments
when unexpected difficulty surprises.
Hard moments
when discouragement blinds vision.
Hard moments
when once again sin rules the heart.
Hard moments
with so many things broken.
Hard moments—
but I am not alone.
Hard moments—
yet I am never left to my limited
     resources.
Hard moments
in your hands become
hard moments of transformation.
Hard moments
in your hands become
hard moments
of amazing grace.

And we know that for those who love God all things work together for good, for those who are called according to his purpose. (Rom. 8:28)

Try to recall a past "hard moment" in your life and consider how God's amazing grace helped you through that time.

Take some time to pray that God will transform today's hard moments in ways that leave you singing his praises.

For further study and encouragement, read 1 Samuel 1–2:10.

Everyone Preaches

Every one of us is a preacher.
We are always preaching
some kind of gospel to
ourselves.
Every one of us is a theologian.
We are always repeating
some kind of belief system to
ourselves.
Every one of us is a philosopher.
We are always discussing
meaning and purpose with
ourselves.
Every one of us is an archaeologist.
We are always digging through
the mound of experiences
that is our life,
making sense of
where we have been,
what we have done,
what you have done, and
who we've been with.
We are always doing this
because we are all
image bearers.
We are created to
think,
interpret,
feel,
know,
desire,
understand,
and worship.
In our seeking to
know
we are searching for
you.
Every one of us is a worshiper
because every one of us is made
for you.
Every one of us is searching
for what can only be found
in you.
So, every one of us needs your
grace.
For there is no life,
there is no hope,
there is no knowing,
that does not begin with
knowing you.

———

But seek first the kingdom of God and his righteousness, and all these things will be added to you. (Matt. 6:33)

What are you searching for?

Have you ever thought of yourself as a preacher, theologian, philosopher, or archaeologist? How might these labels point you to your most important role as a worshiper of God?

For further study and encouragement, read Matthew 7:7–11.

Unfailing Love

I wish I would live with you in view—
eyes to your glory,
ears for your wisdom,
heart for your grace.
But I live with me in view—
eyes to my kingdom,
ears for my opinion,
heart captured by my will.
I know that I was made for you.
I know that hope,
meaning,
purpose,
identity, and
my agenda for every day
is to be found in you.
But I want my own kingdom.
I love my own glory.
I define my own meaning.
I delight in my control.
There's a war that never ends;
the battleground is my heart.
It's a moral skirmish
between what you have ordained
and what I want.
So I don't find pleasure in your glory;
I don't delight in your law.
But my heart doesn't rest.
I know there's a better way.
I know that you are God,
and I am not.

My sin is more than
bad behavior,
bad choices,
or wrong words.
My sin is a violation of the relationship
that I was meant to have with you.
My sin is an act
where I replace you
with something I love more.
Every wrong thing I do
reflects
a lack of love for you, and
reflects
a love of self.
Help me
to see,
to acknowledge,
to weep,
And say,
   "Against you, you only,
         have I sinned
      and done what is evil in
            your sight."
And then, help me to rest
in your mercy,
in your great compassion, and
in your unfailing love
even as the war goes on.

———

You shall love the Lord your God with all your heart and with all your soul and with all your mind. (Matt. 22:37)

Contemplate how "sin is an act where I replace you." How does this definition expand your understanding of sin?

How have you recently been living with yourself "in view" instead of living with God "in view"? Spend some time in prayer, confessing to God and resting in his unfailing love.

For further study and encouragement, read Psalm 51.

Like You

There is no one like
you.
There are no words
to adequately capture the
wonder
of your redeeming power.
There is no one like
you.
No one who knows what you
know.
No one who is able to do what you
do.
You reign over
all that is.
You do with your creation whatever
you want to
do.
No one can question
you.
No one has the power to stop your
hand.
You turn hardship into
rescue.
You turn suffering into
redemption.
Out of trials you bring
transformation.
Out of weakness you grow
strength.

Out of death you birth
life.
Out of darkness you bring
light.
You turn foolishness into
wisdom.
You cause idolaters to bow in
worship.
Every day you create something out
of
nothing.
Every day you make alive what was
once
dead.
Every day you redeem what seems
beyond
redemption.
There is no one like
you.
There are no words
to adequately capture the
wonder
of your redeeming power.
There is no one like
you.
No one who knows what you
know.
No one who is able to do what you
do.

There is none holy like the LORD;
_   there is none besides you;_
_   there is no rock like our God. (1 Sam. 2:2)_

Nearly every line of this poem demonstrates how there is none like God. Work through each statement in the poem and connect it to a real-life example, either from your life or from the Bible, that illustrates the statement. (For example, "You cause idolaters to bow in worship" could refer to a friend turning to Christ for salvation or might describe how Egypt was forced to set the Israelites free.)

Pray your own prayer of praise for all the glorious ways God is like no other.

For further study and encouragement, read
1 Corinthians 1:18–31 and Ezekiel 37:1-14.

Not Like David?

Aren't you glad you're not like David,
such blazoned sin; how could he?
Aren't you glad you're not like Saul,
making up his own rules; what was he thinking?
Aren't you glad you're not like Cain,
violence against his own brother?
Aren't you glad you're not like Rebekah,
such planned deceit?
Aren't you glad you're not like the Israelites,
so easily seduced by idols?
Aren't you glad you're not like Absalom;
how could he be so jealous?
Aren't you glad you're not like Elijah;
how could he forget God and be so depressed?
Aren't you glad you're not like Nebuchadnezzar;
how could he be so obsessed with power?
Aren't you glad you're not like Samson;
how could he be so easily deceived?
Aren't you glad you're not like Jonah;
how could he run from the Father's call?
Aren't you glad you're not like the Pharisees,
so religiously right, yet spiritually wrong?
Aren't you glad you're not like Judas,
selling the Messiah for a little bit of silver?
Aren't you glad you're not like the Corinthians,
so much better at division than at serving the Lord?

But wait.

You are like them, and so am I.
There is simply no denying it.
Their stories are a mirror into which we see ourselves.
We too are jealous and easily deceived.
We too are proud and obsessed with power.

We too are better at division while we run from God.
We too get angry and get seduced by idols.
In sorrow we must say,
we stand with David,
and Saul,
and Rebekah,
and Jonah,
and Elijah,
and the rest.
These stories are for us to look into and see us,
so that we are not able
to buy into
the lie of our own righteousness,
but instead,
run to God's mercy,
hold onto his unfailing love,
and finally rest
in his great compassion.
Aren't you glad you can step out of the darkness of self-deceit
and admit who you are?

———

Pride goes before destruction,
    and a haughty spirit before a fall. (Prov. 16:18)

Are you familiar with the shortcomings of the individuals mentioned
in this poem? If not, find and read their stories in the Bible.

How might you be comparing yourself with others in a way that
incorrectly boosts your self-righteousness?

For further study and encouragement, read 1 Corinthians 10:1-13.

Weak (1)

Today I am very weak—
weak body,
weak heart,
lacking ability,
devoid of resolve,
little anticipation,
waves of discouragement,
whispers of fear,
dreading a sleepless night,
expecting the pain of the morning,
wishing to run,
nowhere to hide,
feeling sentenced to what I cannot survive.
Wondering, "How long?"
Questions—
no answers.
But I have come to understand
that my weakness is a grace,
that hopelessness is not a prison.
Hopelessness is a doorway.
There is no shame in weakness.

I was created weak,
designed to be dependent.
To confess weakness
is to own my humanity.
To own my humanity
is to embrace my need of help.
To embrace my need of help
means to open the door to God's
    warehouse of
protecting,
providing,
comforting,
confronting,
strengthening,
hope-giving, and
motivating grace.
Today I am weak,
but I will boast in my weakness
for when I am weak,
for me, you are strong.

The parts of the body that seem to be weaker are indispensable . . .
(1 Cor. 12:22)

Recall ways that God has supported you during times of physical or emotional weakness.

Are you able to rejoice in your own weakness? Pray for God's help to develop such an attitude.

For further study and encouragement, read 2 Corinthians 12:1-10.

One Thing

One thing,
One thing,
One thing!
It's hard to imagine
one thing
When I seem to be attracted
to so many things.
It is a continuing
struggle.
It is a daily
battle.
It is my constant
war.
The world of the physical
attracts me,
excites me,
magnetizes me, and
addicts me.
I confuse consumption
with satisfaction.
I confuse satisfied senses
with true joy.
I confuse a stomach that is full
with a heart at rest.
Sometimes I would rather have
my appetites satisfied
than a grace-filled heart.
Sometimes I would rather hold
the physical
than have the eyes of my heart
filled with the beauty of
the spiritual.

I am tired of only seeing
what
my physical eyes
can see.
I want eyes
to see
what
cannot be seen.
I am tired of craving
people,
possessions,
locations,
circumstances,
positions,
experiences,
appearances . . .

Somewhere in my heart,
I know that only you
satisfy.
Deep in my heart,
I want you to be
enough.
I must quit
moving,
running,
driving,
pursuing,
consuming.
I need to
stop.
I need to

be quiet.
I need to sit
in the seat of grace
and wait,
and wait,
until these blind eyes
see,
until this cold heart
craves
the one beauty that
satisfies—
the one beauty that
is you.

———

The fear of the Lord leads to life,
*   and whoever has it rests satisfied.*
*   (Prov. 19:23)*

What tends to distract you from the
"one thing"?

What are the differences between
consumption and satisfaction?
Satisfied senses and true joy? Which
word better describes your heart
most days?

For further study and encouragement,
read Psalm 42.

The Rejection of Rejection

Unthinkable,
irrational,
impossible to conceive!
The Trinity
torn asunder.
The Son
wrenched from his Father.
Salvation realized.
I am
the liar.
I am
the thief.
I am
the gossip.
I am
the rebel.
I have wanted
my own way
in
my own time
at
my appointed place.
I have rebelled
against your law
and I have
set up my own.
I deny
your kingship
while building
a kingdom of my own.
I think
my wisdom
is wiser than yours.

I think
my plan
is better than yours.
I crave
the sovereignty
that only you should have.
But you did
the inconceivable;
you accomplished
the undoable.
You stood
in my place
and you satisfied
God's wrath.
But
in the process,
the three in one
was torn in two.
In the process,
the Father
did the most painful thing
that has ever been done.
He turned his back
on you.
You withstood
this pain
so that I would never have to.
You took my
rejection
so that I would only ever have
acceptance.
So that I can
rest assured,

I can
live in hope,
I can
enjoy true peace,
because I know
that you are always with me.
For long ago
on the cross
your rejection
was, for me,
the final rejection of rejection.

———

And about the ninth hour Jesus cried out with a loud voice, saying, "Eli, Eli, lema sabachthani?" that is, "My God, my God, why have you forsaken me?" (Matt. 27:46)

Contemplate the amazing love of Christ that compelled him go to the cross on your behalf.

Christ was rejected for your sins—prayerfully thank him for covering them.

For further study and encouragement, read Isaiah 53.

The Wrong Guys

I think about it all the
time.
It doesn't seem
fair.
It doesn't seem
right.
I try to make the equation work,
but it doesn't.
They don't give you
the time of day.
They couldn't care less
about your law.
They are proud
of their pride.
They are so arrogant
their tongues
strut.

They mock your
existence.
They scoff at your
boundaries.
They not only make threats,
they resort to
violence.
Their boasting is their
bling.
I usually swallow
my questions,
but I'm roaring
inside.
It makes me tired to
think about it,
and it does make
my obedience

seem like a waste.
They seem to have little
trouble.
They seem to seldom
suffer.
But I do!
And while I suffer,
they are
fat and happy.
Then in my
confusion
it hit me.
This is but
a moment,
a dream,
a mist,
a vapor,
a quick passage through
a temporary place.
This is not
my home.
This is a journey
toward home.
They think this is home,
but this is not
home.
Please guide me on
my way.
Please hold me with
your hand.
And when I am
weary
and my heart is about to
fail

and my reserves of strength are
gone,
please help me to
remember
that they have ease and riches
but
I have you,
and you will be my
strength and portion
forever.

———

Truly God is good to Israel,
  to those who are pure in heart.
But as for me, my feet had almost
    stumbled,
  my steps had nearly slipped.
For I was envious of the arrogant
  when I saw the prosperity of the
    wicked. (Ps. 73:1–3)

Do you ever feel as if obeying God
isn't worth it because those who don't
follow him seem to be succeeding?
But what is the error in this sort of
thinking?

How regularly do you remind yourself
that you have not yet reached your
final home?

For further study and encouragement,
read Luke 16:19–31.

Beauty

I need to see your beauty.
I need to remember that you are
beautiful in sovereignty,
beautiful in wisdom,
beautiful in power,
beautiful in mercy,
beautiful in faithfulness,
beautiful in love,
beautiful in patience,
beautiful in holiness,
beautiful in justice, and
beautiful in grace.
It is only when I look at the
trials of my life,
the things unwanted,
the things unplanned,
the things unexpected,
the things that are hard,
through the lens of your
stunning beauty
that I see them with
accuracy and clarity.
But I also need to remember that
grace
has connected me to the beauty that
is you.
By grace all that you are,
you are for me.
So to fight my divine beauty
amnesia,
tomorrow once again in the quiet of
early morning,

I will stop and gaze upon your beauty,
and I will
rest,
remember,
worship, and
celebrate,
knowing that glorious grace has
connected me to the
stunning beauty
that is and forever will be
you.

———

*Finally, brothers, whatever is true,
whatever is honorable, whatever is
just, whatever is pure, whatever is
lovely, whatever is commendable,
if there is any excellence, if there
is anything worthy of praise, think
about these things. (Phil. 4:8)*

Consider your personal trials through
the lens of God's stunning beauty.

What are some habits you can
develop to help you remember that
you are connected to God's beauty
through his grace?

For further study and encouragement,
read Colossians 3:1–17.

Somebody Else

I really wish I could blame
somebody else.
I wish I could place the responsibility
on somebody else.
I would love to point the finger
at somebody else.
I wish I could convince myself
that it was somebody else.
I tried to feed myself the logic
that it was somebody else.
For a moment I bought my argument
that it was somebody else.
There is always another sinner
who can bear my fault.
There is always some circumstance
that can carry my blame.
There's always some factor
that made me do what I did.
There's always somewhere else to
    point
rather than looking at me.
But in the darkness of bedtime,
the logic melts out of my heart.
In the moments before sleep,

the pain begins to squeeze away my
    breath.
As my mind replays the day's
    moments,
the conclusion is like a slap.
There is no monster
to hide from.
There is no excuse that holds.
My war is not external;
the enemy is not outside.
The struggle rages within me—
nowhere to point or run.
No independent righteousness,
no reason for smugness or rest,
I am my greatest enemy
and rescue is my only hope.
In the quiet, I face it.
I cannot blame somebody else.
One more time I close my eyes,
    admitting that
my only hope is found in
Somebody Else.

And there is salvation in no one else, for there is no other name under heaven given among men by which we must be saved. (Acts 4:12)

Are you also tempted to point at others or circumstances when you are to blame?

Do you truly believe your only hope is found in Jesus alone?

For further study and encouragement, read Romans 3.

You Are

You are the
sun that shines in darkness.
You are the
water that quenches thirst.
You are the
balm that heals the wounded.
You are the
Master that calms the storm.
You are the
rose of brightest beauty.
You are the
chosen, perfect Lamb.
You are the
King of a greater kingdom.
You are the
captain of battles won.
You are the
lion of chosen Judah.
You are the
dove of peace that's come.
You are the
shelter for the homeless.
You are the
Father to helpless orphans.
You are the
chosen, suffering Son.
You are
my God,
my Savior,
my hope,
my life,
my forgiveness,
my wisdom,
my strength,
my righteousness,
my peace,
my Father,
my brother,
and my friend.
Because you are,
I am what I am.

———

For who is God, but the LORD?
  And who is a rock, except our God?
This God is my strong refuge
  and has made my way blameless.
    (2 Sam. 22:32–33)

Form your own list of God's glorious
attributes as an act of praise.

Consider how your life is different
because you are God's.

For further study and encouragement,
read Psalm 103.

Forgetful

I was anxious this morning—
too many details,
loose ends,
"what if's"
and "if only's."
Demanding schedule,
depending on people,
deadlines lurking.
Feeling out of control,
inadequate, and
overscheduled.
Worry robs peace.
Doubt plunders faith.
Anxiety decimates rest.

Impatient,
irritable,
demanding,
unloving,
unthankful,
convicted,
remorseful,
confessing.
Worry is forgetful.
Anxiety is a form of
amnesia.
Forgetting
your presence,
your plan,

your wisdom, and
your grace.
What is not under my
control
is never out of
control
because you are with me,
and you control
everything
for your glory
and
for my good.
May I learn to
remember
and,
in remembering,
learn to rest
in the one constant
on which I can always depend—
you.

———

The Lord is at hand; do not be anxious about anything, but in everything by prayer and supplication with thanksgiving let your requests be made known to God. (Phil. 4:5–6)

Do you find it difficult to rest in God during times of busyness and chaos?

Prayerfully offer your worries for today to God.

For further study and encouragement, read Matthew 6:25–34.

Identity Amnesia

Identity amnesia
produces
identity replacement.
It has been
humanity's problem
since
a man and a woman
in a garden
(given as a gift)
attempted to
reach up
for the
place
of Another.

When I look at your heavens, the work of your fingers,
the moon and the stars, which you have set in place,
What is man that you are mindful of him,
and the son of man that you care for him? (Ps. 8:4)

Take some time to contemplate your identity
before God.

What can you do to avoid "identity amnesia" that
often produces "identity replacement"?

For further study and encouragement, read Genesis 3.

Too Much

I envy too much.
Calculating that math of
success and possessions
to see if my resources
add up to more
than others.
I notice too much
when others enjoy
comfort and ease.
I think too much of how
others seem blessed by you.
I analyze too much
the balance sheet of your goodness.
My envy exposes the danger of
my selfish heart.
My envy reveals that I often
    worship me
more than I worship you.
My envy shows I still look for life
where it will never be found.
I still envy too much
so I still need you.
I need what only you can do.
I need the grace only you
can give.
I envy too much
so I still need
what all the things I envy
will never give me.
I still need to be rescued
by you.

———

A tranquil heart gives life to the flesh,
    but envy makes the bones rot.
        (Prov. 14:30)

Do you find yourself envious of
others' prosperity or blessings?

Consider how Christ can rescue you
from the trap of envy.

For further study and encouragement,
read 1 Timothy 6:3-10.

Celebration

It will be
the most exuberant
celebration ever.
It will never grow
boring.
It will always be
fresh.
It will consume us all.
We will want to do
nothing else.
The celebration will go
on and on,
with songs that will never grow
old.
We will be so amazed
that we have been invited into
the choir.
And our amazement will never
abate.
This celebration that will never end
is the celebration of
grace.
If you listen carefully,
you will hear
the songs have already
begun!

_____

You make known to me the path of life;
in your presence there is fullness
of joy;
at your right hand are pleasures
forevermore. (Ps. 16:11)

Allow yourself to ponder the joys of
heaven as you go about your daily
tasks today.

Celebrate and rejoice in the grace
that God has extended to you. Try
to describe it in as much detail as
possible.

For further study and encouragement,
read Revelation 21.

Something in My Hands I Bring

God doesn't want you to come to him empty-handed.
No, you can't come to him full of yourself,
and you can't come to him based on your track record,
and you can't use your performance as a recommendation.
No, you can't come to him based on your family,
your personality,
your education,
your position in life,
the successes you've had,
the possessions you've accumulated,
or the human acceptance you've gained.
But God requires you to come with your hands full.
He requires you to bring to him the sweetest of sacrifices,
the sacrifice of words.
He calls you to bring Hosea's offering:
    "Return, Israel, to the Lord your God.
     Your sins have been your downfall!
     Take words with you
     and return to the Lord.
     Say to him:
    'Forgive all our sins
     and receive us graciously,
     that we may offer the fruit of our lips.'"
God doesn't want you to come to him empty-handed.
He asks of you a sacrifice,
not a grain offering,
not a lamb or a bull.
No, that requirement had been satisfied
by the blood of the Lamb.
Yet God asks of you a sacrifice.
It is the offering of words,
words of humility,

words of honesty,
words of moral courage,
words of moral candor,
words that could only be spoken
by one who rests in grace.
Words of confession are what you must bring.
Place words,
free of negotiation or excuse,
on his altar of grace
and receive forgiveness and cleansing.
Uncover your heart,
exposed by words, and say:
   "We will never again say, 'Our gods'
    to what our own hands have made,
    for in you the fatherless find compassion."
What David willingly did, he requires of you.
Come with words.
It is the way of grace.
It is the way of freedom.
It is the way to God.

_____

You will not delight in sacrifice, or I would give it;
   you will not be pleased with a burnt offering.
The sacrifices of God are a broken spirit:
   a broken and contrite heart, O God, you will not despise. (Ps. 51:16–17)

Contemplate how an "offering of words" is the way of grace and freedom.

Consider and gather up the "words" you can offer as a humble sacrifice to God today.

For further study and encouragement, read Hosea 14.

Not Always

I want to trust you,
but not always.
I want to believe that
your way is the
best way,
but not always.
I want to believe that
you are wisdom,
that I have little,
but not always.
I want to believe that
every boundary you set is
good for me,
but not always.
I have come to love
your law,
but not always.
I have given my heart to
worship the Creator,
but not always.
I have come to
understand
that the weaknesses in
my faith
and the inconsistencies of
my following
daily preach to me
that I am far from

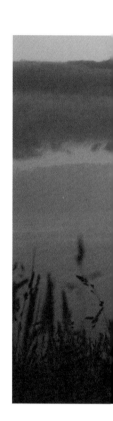

being free of
need for the
insight,
rescue,
forgiveness,
transformation,
empowerment,
deliverance,
and freedom
that only your grace
can give.
Tomorrow I will long to be
faithful,
but will prove to be
inconsistent
once again.
Tomorrow
will not always
still be in my life,
but I have hope,
for I know you will greet me with
convicting love,
forgiving grace, and
renewing power
once again
because with you there is no
"not always."

Restore to me the joy of your salvation,
  and uphold me with a willing spirit. (Ps. 51:12)

Even though we humans are "not always" as consistent in our convictions as we wish to be, how does knowing that God is always the same provide us peace?

Take some time in prayer to confess how you fall short and to praise God for his perfection.

For further study and encouragement, read Mark 14:32–42.

No Question

There is no question
that sin is dangerous.
There is no question
that it produces no good.
There is no question
that it seduces everyone.
There is no question
of its power to deceive.
There is no question
that I am a victim.
There is no question
that I was born in its fold.
There is no question
that I have no power to escape it.
There is no question
that I can't free myself from its hold.
There is no question
that I've chosen what is foolish.
There is no question
that I've loved what is wrong.
There is no question
that I've transgressed your boundaries.
There is no question
that my trespass has been bold.
There is no question
that I deserve your judgment.
There is no question
that I have no righteousness to hold.

So there is no question
that there is any hope outside your
    mercy.
There is no question
that I have any plea but your grace.
There is no question
that your sacrifice is needed.
There is no question
that you hung in my place.
There is no question
that I have nothing to be proud of.
There is no question
that I should boast in your cross.
There is no question
that you are the Lamb that was
    promised.
There is no question
that I am covered by your blood.
There is no question
that I will rest in your promise.
There is no question
that you will bless me with peace.
There is no question
that you will defeat what is in me.
There is no question
that I will finish my journey.
There is no question
that someday I will be free.

———

All we like sheep have gone astray;
*   we have turned—every one—to his own way;*
and the LORD has laid on him
*   the iniquity of us all. (Isa. 53:6)*

How certain are you that the gospel is true?

Turn this poem into a personal prayer of thanksgiving, praising God for the certainty of your salvation.

For further study and encouragement, read Romans 5:12–21.

Mercy Prayer

I have no résumé
to hold before you,
no track record of accomplishments,
no letters of commendation,
no rights of birth or ethnicity.
I hold nothing
that would place you in my debt,
nothing
that could curry your favor,
nothing
that would obligate you.
I wish unbridled zeal
would commend me to you.
I wish unbroken obedience
would draw your attention.
I wish model wisdom and model love
would convince you that I'm worthy.
But I have none of these things
to offer you.
I stand before you with shoulders bent
and hands that are empty.
I approach you with no
argument in my mind
or words to offer in my defense.
I stand before you
naked and undeserving,
broken and weak.
I am quite aware of the
duplicity of my heart,
the evil of my choices,
and the failure of my behavior,

but I am not afraid
because I stand before you
with one argument,
with one plea.
This argument is enough.
This plea is sufficient.
This argument is the only thing
that could ever give me
courage,
rest,
and sturdy hope.
So I come before you
with this plea—
your mercy.
Your mercy is my rest.
Your mercy is my hope.
Your mercy makes me bold.
Your mercy is all I need.
Your mercy
tells me you will hear.
Your mercy
tells me you will act.
Your mercy
tells me you will forgive.
Your mercy
tells me you will restore.
Your mercy
tells me you will strengthen

Your mercy is my
welcome,
plea,
and rescue.
I rest in this one thing:
you are mercy,
and
you will answer.

_____

The Lord is good to all,
*   and his mercy is over all that he*
*   has made. (Ps. 145:9)*

Recall the ways God has been
merciful to you in the past.

Spend some time in prayer, thanking
God for his past mercies and asking
for his grace in current situations.

For further study and encouragement,
read Titus 3:3–7.

Rest

Rest:
a faint dream for many,
a treasured commodity
in a fallen world,
a thing so needed
yet so easily interrupted.
The garden was a place of
rest—
no violence in creation,
no weed or thorn,
no cleft between God and man,
no reason to hide,
no cause for fear,
no need unmet,
no grief to face.
Bright sun,
pure love,
unfettered peace,
unstained beauty,
man and God,
worship and love.
But, a voice
interrupted the rest:
strategies of death,
words of deceit,
actions of rebellion,
fingers of blame,
expulsion from the garden,
judgment and death,
rest interrupted,
rest shattered.
So we wait for the Lord.

His grace strengthens,
his presence comforts,
his promises assure,
his power activates, and
his rule guarantees
that someday rest—
real rest,
pure rest,
eternal rest—
will reign once more.
No violence in creation,
no weed or thorn,
no cleft between God and man,
no reason to hide,
no cause for fear,
no need unmet,
no grief to face
between God and man.
Yes, rest, true rest,
will live again
and last forever.
So we wait for the Lord
to restore us to that place.
Bright Son,
pure love,
unfettered peace,
unstained beauty,
God and man,
together forever.
Until that day,
with hearts
that are strong,

and hope
that is undimmed,
and joy
that embraces the future,
we wait for the Lord.

———

Come to me, all who labor and are
heavy laden, and I will give you rest.
(Matt. 11:28)

Do you have regular time set aside for
rest? If not, consider when you might
be able to work times of rest into
your schedule.

Consider the various ways the fall
has made true rest difficult, both
generally for mankind and personally
for yourself.

For further study and encouragement,
read Hebrews 4:1–13.

When God Is Glad

In the pain
of my confession,
it's hard to recollect
the fleeting pleasures
of my sin.
My shame
hides your face.
My anguish
drowns out your voice.
The lingering visions
of what I've done
haunt
my soul,
assault
my heart, and
dominate
my thoughts.
I want to undo

what
I've done.
I want
to turn back time
so that
my thoughts would be
pure
and my hands would be
clean.
But
lust was born,
and
the deed was done.
I can't undo
what dark pleasure has wrought.
So I come to you
just as I am.
I bow before you

shamed and unclean.
The searching light
of your righteousness
puts fear in my heart
and
reveals more stains than
I ever thought I had.
I bow before you
because I've nowhere else
to go.
I confess to you
because I've no other
hope.
There's no place
to run.
There's no place
to hide.
I can't escape
what I have done.
I can't erase
my stains.
So in my grief
I ask for one thing:
I long
to hear you sing;
I long
to see you rejoice.
For when my ears are graced
with your song
and when I am blessed
by your gladness
and when the angels
celebrate,
then I can be sure
that I've been given

the greatest
of gifts,
the miracle
of miracles,
the thing that only love
could purchase,
the blessing that only love
could offer—
forgiveness.

———

The Lord your God is in your midst,
*   a mighty one who will save;*
he will rejoice over you with gladness;
*   he will quiet you by his love;*
he will exult over you with loud
*   singing. (Zeph. 3:17)*

Do you feel shame for sin today?
Take some time to pray through
those emotions.

Contemplate the strong connections
in this poem between God's love,
forgiveness, and gladness, and then
praise him for the miracle that such
gifts are bestowed on you.

For further study and encouragement,
read Ephesians 1:3–4.

Fearless Forever

In a world that is held
in such deep darkness
where the light of truth
often seems more of a flicker
than a flame—
in a world where
deceit,
dishonesty,
falsehood,
and foolishness
divert and distort
the lives of so many—
in times when a myriad of
voices
say so
much
about so many things,
where confusion seems
readily available
and clarity seems
hard to find—
in a world where opinions
rise to a place
where only truth should be,
and every voice
seems to get an equal hearing
in the constant cacophony
of ten thousand
contradictory voices—
it is a wonderful
and amazing thing
to be able to say

with rest and confidence,
"The Lord is my light!
My heart has been lit
by the illuminating
and protective glory
of his
powerful and transforming grace,
my mind has been renewed
by the luminescent presence
of his truth-guiding
Holy Spirit,
and my life has been guided
down straight paths
by the ever-shining lamp
of his word.
I am not afraid,
but it is not because
I am strong
or wise.
I am not afraid,
but it is not because
I have power
or position.
I am not afraid,
but it is not because
I have health
or wealth.
I am not afraid,
but it is not because
my circumstances
or relationships
are easy.

I am not afraid
for one glorious reason:
I have been lit by the
Lord of light.
In the darkness
of this fallen world,
I no longer walk
in the night,
but I have been given
the light of life.
I am not afraid
because light lives in me.
This one amazing reality
gives me rest;
I have been rescued from
darkness
and transported into the
light,
and I am not afraid."

———

Your word is a lamp to my feet
  and a light to my path. (Ps. 119:105)

Spend some time thinking about
the similiarities between light and
darkness compared to Christ and our
world. It's an illustration we some-
times hear so often that we forget to
consider it fully. Let your thinking on
these things draw you into prayer.

Is anything making you afraid today
or this week? How should you view
fear based on this poem?

For further study and encouragement,
read Philippians 2:12–18.

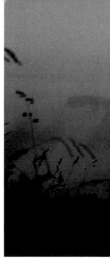

Hearts at Rest

I would like to say
that
my heart is at rest,
but I can't.
I would like to think
that
I always rest in God's care,
but I don't.
I would love to declare
that
my faith is unwavering,
but it isn't.
I wish it was a fact
that
fear is a thing of my past,
but it simply isn't.
It would be nice to know
that
trust's struggle is over,
but it isn't.
I wish I never wanted
to be
my own sovereign,
but I do.
I want to have unbroken rest
in
the hand of God's love,
but I don't.
I long to face difficulty
without
question or doubt,
but I don't.

I do not want to
re-question
my Father's love,
but I do.
I wish I never questioned
the
Lord's good plan,
but I do.
The struggle is better
than
it once was,
but not done.
My rest is more consistent
than
it used to be,
but not complete.
My heart enjoys a greater ease
than
in earlier days of faith,
but unrest comes.
I have lived with you
and
seen your care,
but questions come.
I have seen you do
what
I could not have conceived,
but still I doubt.
I have been in awe
of
the provisions of your grace,
but anxiety comes.

I have submitted myself
to
your will and way,
but still I rebel.
So with rest in your forgiveness
and
confidence in your power,
I come.
With a needy heart
that
craves your help,
I pray:
"Help me, Father, today
to
let go of my need
to always understand.
Enable me to live in rest
when
I don't know
what will happen.
Help me to have a restful heart
when
opposition is great,
and all I have is you."

———

Trust in the Lord with all your heart,
and do not lean on your own
understanding.
In all your ways acknowledge him,
and he will make straight your
paths. (Prov. 3:5–6)

This poem reminds us that each
time we rest in God's faithfulness,
our faith grows. Spend some time
remembering times in the past where
you waited on God and saw him
provide for your needs.

Is there anything you're not resting in
God's hands right now? Pray about
it and ask God for the ability to rest
in him.

For further study and encouragement,
read Psalm 37.

Here

You're not absent,
you're near.
You're not distant,
you're here.
You're not separate,
you hear.
You're not passive,
you reign.
You don't just watch,
you intervene
again,
and again,
and again.
You don't just sit
above what you have created.
No.
You move down among us in
grace,
glory,
wisdom,
power,
and love,
to bestow upon broken creatures
what we could not earn,
what we could not achieve,
and what we'll never deserve.
You step in the mess we created.
You touch what we have broken.
You restore what we have destroyed.
You give life to what we have killed.
You're not absent,
you are near.

You're not distant,
you're here.
You're not separate,
you hear.
You're not passive,
you reign.
You don't just watch us,
you intervene
again,
and again,
and again.

———

The LORD is near to all who call on him,
to all who call on him in truth.
(Ps. 145:18)

How has the Lord been near and
intervening in your life recently?

Take time to consider the love of
Christ, as expressed in his life on
earth and as shared in the blessing of
his Holy Spirit. Let your meditation
flow into prayers of thanksgiving and
worship.

For further study and encouragement,
read Hebrews 4:14–5:10.

In the Way

Care gets in the way of
my worship.
Care gets in the way of
my obedience.
Care gets in the way of
my calling.
Care gets in the way of
acts of sacrifice.
Care gets in the way of
my commitment to love.
Care gets in the way of
thinking what is true.
Care gets in the way of
desiring what is right.
Care gets in the way of
adoring you.
Care gets in the way of
soaking up your truth.
Care gets in the way of
my commitment to peace.
Care gets in the way of
righteous indignation.
Care gets in the way of
your call to be humble.
Care gets in the way of
my service for your kingdom.
It seems like every day,
care gets in the way.
My problem is not that
I care.
My problem is that
I care about me more than

I care about you.
My hope, then, is in the reality that
you care.
You care for me more than
I will ever understand.
In your care is
my assurance that
you will rescue me from the
care that gets in the way.

———

Cast your burden on the Lord,
     and he will sustain you. (Ps. 55:22)

What cares are on your heart and
mind right now? Take some time to
pray about them and leave them in
the Lord's care.

What might be "care" that regularly
distracts you from worship, obedi-
ence, or service for [God's] kingdom?
What practical steps can you take to
make that care less of a distraction?
Offer your cares to the Lord in prayer,
and ask him to help you in this matter.

For further study and encouragement,
read John 14:15–31.

Traces

Traces of your
hand,
traces of your
heart,
traces of your
plan,
traces of your
mercy,
traces of your
power,
traces of your
wisdom,
traces of your
faithfulness,
traces of your
tenderness,
traces of your
forgiveness,
traces of your
sacrifice,
traces of your
rescue,
traces of all
that you are, and
traces of all
that you have done for me
are all over me,
and I will
never, ever again
be what I was
but will be
what only you could make
me be.

Your imprint is
my rescue,
my hope,
my future,
my life,
my fulfillment, and
my redemption.
Your fingerprints are on me,
and I am
glad.

———

But now, O Lᴏʀᴅ, you are our Father;
we are the clay, and you are our
potter;
we are all the work of your hand.
(Isa. 64:8)

Consider the traces of God in
your life. How has knowing him
changed you?

How can you praise him for his work
in you today?

For further study and encourage-
ment, read Ezekiel 36:22–38 and
2 Corinthians 5:16–21.

Weak (2)

I long to be strong,
full of vitality
with energy to spare,
wide awake
with my brain in gear,
spiritually ready,
heart motivated,
purposed possessed,
raring to go
with unstoppable zeal,
a competitor,
a completer,
the envy of others with
no frailties,
no worries, and
no regrets.
But you have rendered me weak,
unable to be what I once was
ever again,
not in this life.
The old me—
gone.
I cannot live as I once did.
I cannot do what I once did.
I cannot press through
what you have chosen for me.
I cannot escape.
I cannot break free.
I cannot will for something better.
Weakness is my lot;
suffering is my prison.
You have chained me to frailty;
I cannot break free.

But this prison is your workroom,
and I am your clay.
You are not a jailer;
you are a potter.
I have not been condemned;
I am being molded.
Your hands have been heavy;
your push on me is hard.
When the soil is resistant,
the molding is violent.
My weakness is not about what I am
enduring.
My weakness is about what I am
becoming.
My travail does not preach your
anger.
My travail preaches your
grace.
This prison is your classroom.
I am learning
your presence.
I am learning
your promises.
I am learning
your power.
I am learning
your mercy.
I am learning
your gospel.
I am learning,
learning,
learning.

The danger for me was never
weakness.
The danger has always been
my delusions of
strength.
You have shattered my delusion
and, in shattering, have proven that
my strength is and always has been
you.

———

My flesh and my heart may fail,
*   but God is the strength of my heart and my portion forever.*
*   (Ps. 73:26)*

What are some weaknesses or sufferings you regularly wish were
lifted from you?

How do these particular weaknesses or sufferings force you to trust
God for strength?

For further study and encouragement, read Isaiah 40:28–31 and
2 Corinthians 12:7–10.

A Light in His Hands

So little preparation,
so many
unrealistic expectations.
So often
dreams are dashed, and
unwanted fears
unrealized.
Too few
understand where they are.
Too few
know where they are going.
Too many
feel alone and lost.
Yet the one who knows
and who understands
has joined the journey.
He holds a light
in his hands,
and he is the one
who can be trusted.

———

Again Jesus spoke to them, saying, "I am the light of the world. Whoever follows me will not walk in darkness, but will have the light of life." (John 8:12)

How easily do you turn to Christ to shed light in your life during confusing times?

Are you ever burdened to share his light with others who are unaware of his help? Who do you know that needs the light and help of Christ?

For further study and encouragement, read John 1.

The Good Life

Easy to be
passive.
Easy to avoid
involvement.
Easy to
look the other way.
Easy to shut up
your heart.
Easy to focus on
me and mine.
Easy to withhold
compassion.
Easy to
shut the door and close the blinds.
Easy to love
what is lovely.
Easy to give to
what will bring a return.
Easy to build a fence around
your comfort
too high to see over
with no gate for an exit.
Easy to sit in the middle
and call it "the good life."

———

Do not be slothful in zeal, be fervent in spirit, serve the Lord. (Rom. 12:11)

What do you think is so easy and comforting about taking a passive or middle road?

Who or what might be hovering just outside of your focus on "me and mine" that needs your Christlike love and attention? What's stopping you from helping?

For further study and encouragement, read Matthew 7:21-23 and Revelation 3:14-22.

Black Friday

There was only one Black Friday.
It was not the day after Thanksgiving.
It was not a day when self-oriented consumers
bumped into,
climbed over,
pushed into,
screamed at,
and hated the other consumers who were
in their way.
No, all the action of the one Black Friday
was on a hill of death
outside the city
where three souls hung on crosses
—two criminals and the Messiah.
Christ doing what he came to do
and what the world was desperate for.
That Friday the world went dark,
the Father turned his back,
graves opened, and
the veil ripped in two.
The Son carried the Father's anger.

Death was offered so life could be given.
Darkness fell so light would shine.
Payment made;
freedom given;
redemption accomplished.
There was only one Black Friday.
No need to shop anymore for
a Savior.

———

For Christ also suffered once for sins, the righteous for the
unrighteous, that he might bring us to God. (1 Pet. 3:18)

Do you ever confuse "Black Friday" and "Good Friday"?
Think through the similarities and differences of these two Fridays.

Spend some time thanking God for the sacrifice of his Son.

For further study and encouragement, read Luke 23:26-50.

The City

The city that surrounds me
seems broken beyond repair.
Lost ones wander the streets;
evil lurks in the alleys.
Sadness afflicts households;
grief omits no one.
Labor does not satisfy;
victories seem short at best.
Satisfaction evades the hungry;
contentment fades away.
But there's a city that is coming;
grace has written my name there.
The right to enter, earned by no one;
the right to stay, no one deserves.
The Son is the gate of entry;
his blood the price that was paid.
That city gives hope to my journey.
That city brings comfort to my care.
That city awakens me in the morning.
That city gives strength for the day.
That city gives answers to my questions.
That city gives reason to my efforts.
That city gives rest when I'm weary.
That city gives me peace to sleep.
I was made for that city.

But as it is, they desire a better country, that is, a heavenly one. Therefore God is not ashamed to be called their God, for he has prepared for them a city. (Heb. 11:16)

Are you feeling depressed by the brokenness of the world around you? Offer those things in prayer to God.

How can remembering the coming of a God-given, grace-filled, eternal city be a source of encouragement to you?

For further study and encouragement, read Revelation 21.

Immanent Sovereignty

You are not a distant Lord,
or a detached Master,
moving the pawns
on the board
in an impersonal act
of winning.
Your lordship
does not separate
me from you
as a serf
would be separated
from a king.
No, you accomplished
your sovereign plan
by invading my
dark and messy world
in the person
of your Son,
giving yourself
in radical grace
to people
who saw no value
in your nearness.
You are Master,
and you are
Immanuel.

You are Lord,
and you are
Father.
You are King,
and you are
Friend.
You are Sovereign,
and you are
Shepherd.
Your rule is not from
afar.
No, your rule brings you
near.

I have hope today
because you are not
distant.
And I celebrate
the amazing
rest and strength
to be found in the reality that
your sovereignty
has brought you
near.

———

All this took place to fulfill what the Lord has spoken by the prophet:

> *"Behold, the virgin shall conceive and bear a son,*
>   *and they shall call his name Immanuel"*

(which means, God with us). (Matt. 1:22–23)

This poem compares and contrasts some different titles and roles of God. Spend some time pondering the list, supplementing it with titles and roles that were not listed. Let this excerise lead you into worship over the many facets of God's character.

Recall or journal about times when God has drawn near to his people (both in the Bible and in your own experiences).

For further study and encouragement, read Philippians 2:1–11.

Spiritual Schizophrenia

It's the schizophrenia of a wandering heart.
It's the contradiction of self-righteousness.
It's the twisted logic of selfishness.
It's something that lurks inside of me.
I wish it wasn't there.
I wish I could say that my heart was free.
I wish my mind was clear and this struggle was over,
but with a guilty conscience
and a broken heart,
I must confess
that I so often look at others through the lens of
the law,
while I want others to look at me through the lens of
grace.
It is a massive contradiction that I look condemningly
at others
while I constantly appeal to you for
grace.
So often when I am greeted with the
weaknesses,
failures,
inconsistencies,
selfishness,
and sins of others,
I respond more as a prosecutor than a
tool of your mercy.
When someone disappoints me,
I tend to run to
your law
instead of taking them to
your cross.
If for just one day you did this
to me,

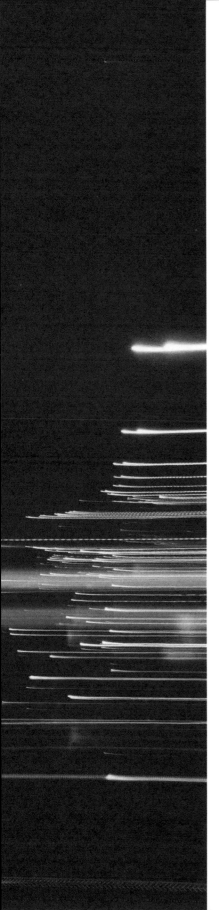

if for just one day
you suspended
your mercy
and all I had was the standard of
your law,
I could not possibly sustain
your judgment.
So, I pray that you would soften my heart.
Help me to see the weight of my sin.
Help me to be broken by the extent of your mercy,
so that the cells of my heart
would be dyed with your grace.
For I am sure that no one gives mercy better
than the one who has come to daily confess
that his only hope in life and death is
your mercy.

———

*Be kind to one another, tenderhearted, forgiving one
another, as God in Christ forgave you. (Eph. 4:32)*

How do you generally respond to people's failures?
How could your response be more Christlike?

How do you respond to your own failures? What might
be a more faithful response?

For further study and encouragement, read
Matthew 18:21–35.

Grace

Your grace is a
cool drink,
warm welcome,
legal defense,
needed warning,
substitute sacrifice,
motivating hope,
warming sun,
welcomed rain,
loving whisper,
humbling confrontation,
guaranteed future,
ultimate gift,
fine meal,
corrective surgery,
heart therapy,
restful oasis,
constant comfort,
promised destiny,
need fulfillment,
sure contentment,
battle won.
All that the law exposes—
my wandering desires,
my fickle heart,
my disloyal eyes,
my sinful lust,
my doubting mind,
my misplaced worship,
my selfish entitlement,
my false righteousness,
my stubborn independence,
my moral failure,
my boundary breaking—
and all the ways I fall short,
your grace, and only
your grace,
forgives,
rescues,
transforms,
and delivers.
You are the best food.
You give the best welcome.
You satisfy.
You fulfill.
It is you, and only you, that I
need.
It is on you only that I
feed.

———

For all have sinned and fall short of the glory of God, and are justified
by his grace as a gift, through the redemption that is in Christ Jesus.
(Rom. 3:23–24)

In this poem, "warming sun," "cool drink," and "loving whisper"
are used to describe God's grace. What creative metaphors can you
add for describing God's grace?

How does the law reveal your sins? Have you confessed them to
God recently and received his grace?

For further study and encouragement, read Romans 7:7–25.

Tired

I was very tired today—
tired of the travail,
tired of trying and failing,
tired of relationships broken,
tired of promises unfulfilled,
tired of hopes evaporating,
tired of dreams dying,
tired of meaningless "I love you's,"
tired of body inability,
tired of heart weakness,
tired of hoping . . .
praying . . .
trying . . .
committing . . .
longing . . .
confessing . . .
repenting . . .
working . . .
and failing.
Today I am tired,
but I have not forgotten
that you never tire.
You are never discouraged.
You are never "at the end of your rope."
You never long to quit.
You never want to "move on."
You never regret what you have done.
You never hope to do better.
You are never caught up short.
You are never weak.
You are never surprised.
You never wish you'd done better.

You are not like me,
and that is very good news.
When I am tired
I remember you,
and once again I tell myself
that you are not like me,
and all
that you are,
you are for me
by grace.

———

My soul melts away for sorrow;
*   strengthen me according to your word! (Ps. 119:28)*

Are you tired today? What makes you weary?

Consider how God himself is able to overcome the things that make us weary, simply because he is God. Let your thoughts turn to praise for the ways he is not like us and for his willingness to support us when we are tired.

For further study and encouragement, read Psalm 121.

Nathan's Legacy

No shouts.
No pointed fingers.
No flashing eyes.
No red-faced accusations.
No inflammatory vocabulary.
No bulging forehead veins.
No derogatory names.
No scary threats.
No arrows of guilt.
No cornering logic.
No "How dare you?"
No "I can't believe you would!"
No "What were you thinking?"
No public confrontation.
No published rebuke.
No arrest warrant.
No handcuffs.
No leading away to be charged.
No list of crimes.
No human tricks.
No trying to do God's work.
No hope of forcing a turning.
No confidence in the power of man.
No human manipulation.
No political posturing.
No, none of these.
Just a humble prophet
telling a simple story—
a sinner with a sinner,
not standing above, but
alongside, together—
wanting to be an instrument,

hoping to assist a blind man to see.
No trust in self,
speaking calmly,
speaking simply,
and letting God
do, through a familiar example
painted with plain words,
what only God can do:
crack the hard-shell heart
of a wayward man
and make it feel again,
see again,
cry again,
pray again,
plead again,
hope again,
love again, and
commit again
to a new and better way.
Not the legacy of
self-righteous,
impatient,
condemning,
"I'm better than you"
anger,
but the harvest
of a man of grace
giving grace
to a man
who doesn't deserve grace,
but won't live again
without it.

And the Lord's servant must not be quarrelsome but kind to everyone, able to teach, patiently enduring evil, correcting his opponents with gentleness. God may perhaps grant them repentance leading to a knowledge of the truth, and they may come to their senses and escape from the snare of the devil, after being captured by him to do his will. (2 Tim. 2:24–26)

When someone has done wrong, how do you react? Do you react as Nathan did?

What focus, as exhibited by Nathan, should you adopt for the next time you need to correct a brother or sister in Christ?

For further study and encouragement, read 2 Samuel 12.

Wanting

It is the deepest disease,
the disastrous delusion,
the insane quest,
the foolish hope,
the universal tragedy.
It cannot be avoided;
no one is able to escape.
We are not wise enough,
pure enough,
strong enough,
submissive enough, or
humble enough.
We are born longing
for what we cannot,
should not,
must not, and
will not
ever have.
We come into this world
wanting to be kings,
working to construct kingdoms of our
    own,

wanting to be in the center,
wanting glory all our own,
wanting to sit on the throne
reserved for you.
We defend our autonomy;
we believe in our sufficiency;
we live independently;
we ignore our true identity.
It is sin's sad legacy,
written deep in history,
capturing all humanity.
There is no rescue,
no escape,
no neat way out
but you.
You came as
manger infant,
suffering servant,
dying substitute,
pleasing Son,
perfect friend,
righteous life,

victory in death,
as a king to be a king.
You would have no physical throne,
no palace guard,
no adoring court,
no political power.
You would establish something
    greater—
a better kingdom,
a better throne,
a greater glory.
You would set up your kingdom
in our hearts,
satisfy us with your reign,
envelop us in your glory.
Our kingship
is our doom.
Your throne
is our hope.
It is for your glory.
It is for our good,
and we are thankful.

——

The Lord *is my shepherd; I shall not*
    want.
    He makes me lie down in green
        pastures.
He leads me beside still waters.
    He restores my soul.
He leads me in paths of righteousness
    for his name's sake. (Ps. 23:1–3)

In what ways are you currently trying
to construct your own kingdom? How
might this demonstrate sin and a lack
of trust in God?

Ponder how something for God's
glory "is for our good." Do you
believe this?

For further study and encouragement,
read Genesis 11:1–9.

Run and Hide

When it all becomes
confusing,
when what is good
seems not so
clear,
when wrong seems
like it's
winning,
where do you
run,
where do you
hide?
When you wonder
if it's worth it to
honor,
worship,
fear, and
obey,
where do you
run,
where do you
hide?

When disappointment
surrounds you
and weariness sets in,
where do you
run,
where do you
hide?
When your soul
is growing
bitter
and your heart is at its
end,
where do you
run,
where do you hide?
When evil seems to
prosper and good suffers
again,
where do you
run,
where do you
hide?

When my flesh is
weak
and my heart may
fail,
there is one thing I have
learned—
you are the only place of
refuge;
you are the only place to
hide.
You are
counsel,
guidance,
glory,
and strength.
I have nothing besides
you.
So in the darkness of
confusion
when I need a place to
hide,
I run to the only place to
hide.
I run to
you.

———

You are my hiding place and my
    shield;
     I hope in your word. (Ps. 119:114)

When you are confused, disappointed,
weary, or bitter, where do you run
and hide? How do places of refuge
that are not God eventually fail us?

Form a list of all the ways that God
is ultimately the best hiding place
for you. Don't forget to include past
personal experiences in the list.

For further study and encouragement,
read 1 Kings 19.

Boast in You

I have taken an accounting
long needed,
long overdue,
humbling,
convicting,
heart-correcting.
I had to admit
that in many ways—
subtle sometimes,
boldly other times—
I have taken personal credit
for what I could not
conceive,
produce,
achieve,
or accomplish on my own.
I have no independent
successes,
accomplishments,
attainments,
prizes,
or positions
that I have manufactured
on my own.
There is nothing that I have done
in my own strength.
There is no ability that I have
    employed
that does not come from
you.
All the things around me
that had to be in place
for me to do

what I have done
exist under your sovereignty,
not my own.
All the people that have
mentored me,
assisted me,
advised me,
cooperated with me,
employed me,
loved me,
guided me,
rescued me,
taught me,
supported me,
stood with me,
stood against me,
cared for me,
protected me, or
worked with me
came into my life
brought there by
you.
I have arrived at places
that were not in my plan.
I have done things
I never envisioned to do.
I have lived in situations
that were not of my wise choosing.
I have been regularly surprised
by the turnings
of my own story.
I have not had the
character,

will,
wisdom,
ambition,
courage,
patience,
commitment,
perseverance,
humility,
discipline,
contentment,
or vision
of a hero.
As I have taken an
accounting,
this is the sum:
there is only one hero in my story;
only one who deserves
credit,
honor,
celebration,
esteem,
and praise.
Clearly that hero is
you.
My successes are the result of
your sovereignty,
your generosity,
your faithfulness,
and your grace.
You are the
author,
expediter,
and completer of my story.

There is nothing
that I have done
that could be done without
you.
There is no reason for me to
boast.
The account points me here—
if I am to boast,
I will boast in
you.

———

Thus says the Lord: "Let not the wise man boast in his wisdom, let not the mighty man boast in his might, let not the rich man boast in his riches, but let him who boasts boast in this, that he understand and knows me, that I am the Lord who practices steadfast love, justice, and righteousness in the earth. For in these things I delight, declares the Lord." (Jer. 9:23–24)

How have you been tempted to take personal credit when it is rightly due to God?

What can you boast of in the Lord today?

For further study and encouragement, read Psalm 34.

Judgment Day

To transgressing of your boundaries,
you will put an end.
To human thoughts of autonomy,
you will put an end.
To delusions of self-sufficiency,
you will put an end.
Grace forbids these going on forever.

To acts of violence and deeds of greed,
you will put an end.
To the burn of lust,
you will put an end.
To injustice and inhumanity,
you will put an end.
Grace prohibits these going on
    forever.

To the silent writing of my own law,
you will put an end.
To using others for personal pleasure,
you will put an end.
To robbing you of divine glory,
you will put an end.
Grace won't tolerate these going on
    forever.

To disobedience to parents,
you will put an end.
To gossip and slander,
you will put an end.
To the worship of comfort,
you will put an end.
Grace wars against these going on
    forever.

To self-aggrandizing pride,
you will put an end.
To self-oriented envy,
you will put an end.
To subtle daily idolatries,
you will put an end.
Grace will not permit these going on
    forever.

To desire-driven lawlessness,
you will put an end.
To attempts at self-sovereignty,
you will put an end.
To denial of what is true,
you will put an end.
Grace restricts these going on forever.

To denial of you and the elevation of
    self,
you will put an end.
To mockery of what is good,
you will put an end.
To the love of what is foolish,
you will put an end.
Grace will not allow these going on
    forever.

What is now will not go on
forever.
This world is marching toward
an end.
We can embrace the hope of
justice.
Final judgment is coming.
Grace requires evil to die forever.

Those far from you will
perish.
Those unfaithful to you will
come to an end.
I have been unfaithful to you.
I have chosen to be far from you.
I have broken each of your laws.
But I am not afraid of what
you will put to an end.
Grace has drawn me near to you.
Grace has paid for my unfaithfulness.
Grace has made me clean in your eyes.
Grace put my stripes on Jesus,
so I would not face them
when you put what-is-now
to an end.

———

*When justice is done, it is a joy to the
        righteous
        but terror to evildoers. (Prov. 21:15)*

What sins of yours will come to an
end in the end?

When you ponder God's justice, what
emotions do you experience? Offer
them in prayer before God.

For further study and encouragement,
read Isaiah 42:1–9.

The Worship of Another

Sacrifices—
I don't want to have to make
sacrifices.
I want my plate
full
and my schedule
empty.
I want to be with people
I like,
people who are low in
maintenance and high in
appreciation.
I want control over
my time,
my energy,
my money, and
my things.
I want my days to be
predictable
and my plans
unobstructed.
I want to experience
success
and successfully avoid
failure.
I would rather be served than
serve.
I would rather get the gift than
give.
I guess this all points me to
one stunning reality:
there is never a day when
my life is
idol free.
There is never a week
when I don't give myself to the
    worship
of another.
It is sad to say
and humbling to admit,
that the chief of these
false deities
is none other than
me.
I am the sovereign
I want to serve.

I am the king
I want others to obey.
I am the lord
I want to rule my days.
Yes, it is true.
"Dear Father,
I want to be
you.
My dissatisfaction is not because
you are not
wise,
faithful,
loving,
and good,
but because I do not get
my own way.
So once more I
bow,
once more I make my
confession,
once more I plead for
mercy,
pardon,
power, and
deliverance."
Once more I ask,
"Dear Savior,
please free me
from me
and cause this selfish heart
to find
joy,

satisfaction,
motivation,
and delight
in doing the
one thing
I was given breath
to do—
to offer myself as a
sacrifice
in the service of
you."

———

*For you were called to freedom,
brothers. Only do not use your
freedom as an opportunity for the
flesh, but through love serve one
another. (Gal. 5:13)*

It can be so easy to slip into a practice
of serving yourself. What areas of
self-service have you slipped into
recently?

How can you offer yourself "as a
sacrifice in the service" of Christ
today?

For further study and encouragement,
read Romans 12.

Two Words You Never Want to Hear

It is such a comfort
to me,
such a source
of hope
and strength
and daily joy.
It gives me reason
to get up in the morning
and to press on
even
when I am discouraged
and weak
and lonely
and afraid.
It gives me reason
to face with courage
the struggles within
and the difficulties without.
It reminds me
that I can stand
before you
as I am,
completely unafraid,
and ask of you
what I have asked before
and will ask again—
your forgiveness
and your help.
What gives me this
courage?
What offers me this
hope?

It is this one thing:
I know for certain
that there are
two words
that I'll never hear.
I know that you will never
look me in the eye
and say to me,
"Go away!"
You will not send me
from your presence.
You will not drive me
from your grace.
You will not separate me
from your glory.
You will not eliminate me
from your promises.
You will never
ever
ever
send me away.
Because your anger
was borne by Another.
Because my separation
was carried by him.
Because he was
sent away,
I will never be.
So in weakness,
failure,
foolishness,
and sin,

I stand before you once more
with courage,
hope,
comfort,
and joy,
because I know
that in all the
dark things that
may be whispered to me
in this dark and fallen world,
there are two words I will never hear.
And so with gratitude and joy
I get up to face the day.
But as I do, I do it
without fear.

———

For he has said, "I will never leave
you nor forsake you." So we can
confidently say,

> *"The Lord is my helper;*
> *I will not fear . . ." (Heb. 13:5–6)*

Have you ever pondered that you will
never hear the words "go away" from
God? What sort of emotions does this
truth bring you?

Spend some time in prayer, praising
God for his faithfulness.

For further study and encouragement,
read 1 John 4.

Moral Vulnerability

Beauty compelling
tugging, seducing,
wanting, and craving
weakened resolve.

Lingering, staring
moral transgression
look of desire
selfish rebellion
act of betrayal
weakened resolve.

Long consideration
dreams of possessing
evil hoping
enemy lurking
heart now racing
battle raging
nervous thinking
flesh growing weaker
drawn to the darkness
weakened resolve.

Wrong seen as righteous
plausible lies
twisted pretenses
self swindling
guilty logic
deluded perspectives
weakened resolve.

Deciding and choosing
date and location
concrete plans
words of acceptance
verbal contract
shared deception
anticipation
tracks covered over
weakened resolve.

Deed now accomplished
fleeing the scene
dark of night
trembling hands
afraid of discovery
made-up stories
weakened resolve.

Morning remorse
hard to imagine
fear of discovery
rehearsed denials
lust unweakening
purity lost
no undoing
weakened resolve.

Protecting secrets
telling lies
acting the part
believable excuses
internal battles
hunger for more
weakened resolve.

Haunted by guilt
crushed by conviction
no more delusion
power of truth
weakened resolve.

Stain of iniquity
remorse of transgression
cries for forgiveness
hope for mercy
cast on compassion
admission of guilt
weakened resolve.

Bitter harvest
sweet forgiveness
the grace of cleansing
joy in acceptance
rescuing Savior
loving Redeemer
patient Father
acting in power
sin's bondage broken
no more compulsion
freedom is given
weakened resolve.

Confession of weakness
tell of his mercy
worship and service
willing obedience
resisting temptation

Seeking assistance
sacrifice gladly
witness to battle
praise and thanksgiving
long perseverance
gone is deception
weakened resolve.

———

*But I say to you that everyone who
looks at a woman with lustful intent
has already committed adultery with
her in his heart. (Matt. 5:28)*

This poem portrays the deepening
degrees of succumbing to temptation—
what phases or stages do you observe
in it? Do they match what you've
observed in your own life for any type
of sin (lust-driven or not) that you've
struggled against?

What emotions did you feel the
last time you succumbed to sin and
then finally confessed and sought
forgiveness?

For further study and encouragement,
read Proverbs 5.

Need

I don't need
a crystal ball,
a fortune teller,
a deck of cards,
a charismatic prophet, or
a look at the tea leaves.
I don't need
to obsess about what's
around the corner,
down the road, or
about to surprise me.
I don't need to fear
the unplanned,
the unexpected, or
the unwanted.
I don't need to
live in the future,
worry about what's not yet, or
try to figure out divine secrets.
I don't need to
try to control what I can't control.
I don't need to
wish I could understand what I can't
    understand
or be paralyzed by what's unknown.

I can live in the moment,
fight today's battles,
surrender my heart,
love my neighbor,
worship, and serve.
I have been blessed by rest—

rest that comes
not from figuring out the future,
deducing what is coming, and
solving future mysteries.
No, I rest because the one
who has everything figured out
is my Father,
and he holds me and my future
in the hollow of his hand.

———

And my God will supply every need of
yours according to his riches in glory
in Christ Jesus. (Phil. 4:19)

Do you find yourself trying to
"control what [you] can't control"?

Do you believe that God "has every-
thing figured out"? Spend some time
praising him for who he is, how he's
cared for you, and how he'll continue
to provide for you.

For further study and encouragement,
read Matthew 6:25–34.

Walk Away

I argued when I should've listened.
I walked away with anger in my heart.
It happened again.
I said words not to be said.
I flashed with irritation not to be felt.
But you didn't leave me to myself.
Unlike me, you didn't get angry and
    walk away.
You drew near and plagued my
    conscience
with a pain I couldn't
escape,
deny,
rationalize,
or avoid.
You weren't irritated with me.
You weren't steaming with impatience.
You weren't landing a blow to hurt.
You weren't punishing me.
No, you were blessing me with grace.
The immediate pursuit of your Spirit
    was
rescue,
conviction,
restraint,
and forgiveness.
It is an amazing and blessed thing.
Again and again you have done this.
When I am in trouble,
in boundless love you trouble me with
    your grace
until I confess my trouble
and run once again to you for
mercy.

—

My son, do not despise the Lord's
    discipline
    or be weary of his reproof.
for the Lord reproves him whom he
    loves,
    as a father the son in whom he
    delights. (Prov. 3:11–12)

Is the Holy Spirit pricking your
conscience about anything today?

How has the Holy Spirit "plagued
[your] conscience" in the past in ways
that you're grateful for now?

For further study and encouragement,
read Hebrews 12:3–11.

The Shoulders of Jesus

Brightest night,
darkest day,
shining star,
midday gloom,
celebratory angels,
grieving loved ones.

Messiah child,
cross-hung criminal,
life of promise,
shocking sacrifice.
Shepherds worship.
Disciples hide.

Peace mission,
bloody injustice,
magi adoration,
soldiers mocking,
perfect man,
convict's demise.

Holy one hangs,
veil torn in two,
giver of life,
public death,
pleasing Son,
Father turns away.

Light collides with darkness.
Graces smashes into injustice.
New birth grows out of sacrifice.
Babe on a death mission,
God on a mercy plan.
Bethlehem gives birth to Calvary.
Death unlocks eternity.
Rejection gifts acceptance.

Redemption's paradox
all lovingly carried
on the shoulders of Jesus.

———

*Behold, the Lamb of God, who takes
away the sin of the world! (John 1:29)*

Have you ever contemplated the
paradox of the birth and death of
Christ? What do you find most
amazing?

Spend some time meditating on the
different terms and phrases describ-
ing both Christ's birth and death. Let
your thoughts lead you into worship-
ful prayer.

For further study and encouragement,
read Luke 2:25–38.

Tough Moments

In those tough moments
when I'm facing
the unexpected,
the unwanted,
the hard,
the sad,
the confusing,
and the difficult,
it is easy for me to
forget
that the hard hammer of
trial
in your hands is a
tool
of redeeming grace.
In those hard moments
I am not being beaten for my
sin
but reshaped by your
grace.
You have already carried my
punishment,
so all that you plan for
me
is an expression of your
unrelenting,
undeserved,
unfathomable,
redeeming
love.

―――――

*We rejoice in our sufferings, knowing
that suffering produces endurance,
and endurance produces character,
and character produces hope, and
hope does not put us to shame, because
God's love has been poured into our
hearts through the Holy Spirit who has
been given to us. (Rom. 5:3–5)*

What is a trial you've gone through
that demonstrated God's redeeming
grace, now that you can look back
on it?

What trial are you experiencing right
now? How might God be showing
you grace in the midst of your present
trouble?

For further study and encouragement,
read James 1:2-18.

Secret Wish

Perhaps
it's a secret wish
of every soul
struggling in the middle
of what he did not plan
and did not choose.

Perhaps
it's the silent cry
of each of us
as we are forced to deal
with someone
who is difficult to love.

Perhaps
we all think that
we're wiser than we really are
and more benevolent
than we would actually be.

Perhaps
we all forget that
sin has reduced us to fools
and shrunk our field of interest
to the size of our own needs.

Perhaps
that's why all of us
secretly wish to be
sovereign.

—————

Do nothing from selfish ambition or conceit, but in humility count others more significant than yourselves. Let each of you look not only to his own interests, but also to the interests of others. (Phil. 2:3–4)

What ways are you likely to forget humility?

Why should we be humble?

For further study and encouragement, read Daniel 4.

Awake Again

Awake again,
knowledge of another day
like the previous,
authored
by the pen of Another.
My own narrative
unknown to me
before
the chapters unfold.
Things to be faced
unknown
before
I face them.
Dreams come
of prophetic vision,
more power,
greater control.
In a world broken
with people flawed,
in the middle
of daily mystery
where questions multiply
and answers flee,
it is a constant battle
to accept
your limits.

————

Your eyes saw my unformed substance;
in your book were written, every one of
  them,
    the days that were formed for me,
    when as yet there was none of
      them.
How precious to me are your thoughts,
    O God!
    How vast is the sum of them!
If I would count them, they are more
    than the sand.
    I awake, and I am still with you.
    (Ps. 139:16–18)

What unknowns or uncertainties are
worrying you today? Offer them in
prayer to God.

How and why can you have faith in
the midst of confusion?

For further study and encouragement,
read Psalm 77.

God's Pleasure

I must admit
I am embarrassed
by
what gives me
pleasure.
It doesn't take
much
to make me
smile.
I get
real pleasure
from
a good steak,
nice chocolate, or
a comfortable
bed.
I want the joy
of
cold soda
and
hot tea.
I want the bathroom
to
be empty when
I need it.
I want the streets
I drive on
to
be free of other
drivers.
I want people
to
respect my opinions
and
validate my plans.
I want my wife
to
be satisfied
with me as
I am.

I want
my bills all
paid
and plenty of money
to
do pleasurable
things
that make me
happy.

But God
isn't like
me.
His pleasures
aren't a sad
catalog
of
low-grade
idolatries.
His desires
aren't shaped
by
ravenous self-focus.
He
doesn't
live
in a perpetual state
of
self-absorbed
discontent.
His pleasures
are never
regrettable

ugly
or
unholy.
When
God smiles,
his reason
is holy
and his purpose
is
pure.
He finds
great pleasure
in his glory
and
great joy
when
the repentant
turn
from the pursuit
of
their own glory and
turn
toward his.
He has
great pleasure
in
the success
of
his plan
and finds
satisfaction
in seeing

his children
turn
from their pleasure
to
live for
his.

Someday
by his grace
the pleasures
that give me
pleasure
will be
the things that
please God.
Until then,
my
hope is in the
fact
that he finds
delight
in rescuing those
who
have been led
astray
by their pleasures,
because
once more today
I'm
going to need
that rescue.

And I'll need
it
every day until
my
deepest pleasures
are nowhere to be found
in
creation
and only to be found
in
the Creator.

———

*Indeed, I count everything as loss
because of the surpassing worth
of knowing Christ Jesus my Lord.
(Phil. 3:8)*

What are the good pleasures you
enjoy?

How can you begin to elevate God's
pleasure above these good things?

For further study and encouragement,
read Philippians 3:8–21.

Thankful

I am so thankful
that on my loneliest day
I am not alone—
you are with me.
I am so grateful
that in my very weakest moment
I am not left to my weakness—
you are my strength.
I am so amazed
that when I am most foolish
(I am cursed to be foolish)—
you are my wisdom.
It is incredible to me
that when my life is out of control—
you control it all for me.
It is a joy to me
that when I am my most unrighteous,
I am not left to my unrighteousness—
you are my righteousness.
I enjoy such peace
because what I am not—
by grace you are for me,
right here, right now,
and for all the
right here's and right now's
that are to come.

_____

*Trust in the L*ORD *with all your heart,*
and do not lean on your own
understanding.
In all your ways acknowledge him,
and he will make straight your
paths. (Prov. 3:5-6)

How are you and God different?
Spend some time in prayer thanking
God for being what you are not.

What is an example from your own
life of how God covers your failures?

For further study and encouragement,
read 2 Timothy 2:11-13.

Legacy

It's impossible not to.
It will happen
somehow,
some way.
I will leave a
trail
behind me.
I will leave a
well-traveled pathway with
footprints
for others to
follow.
Footprints of
relationships,
values,
character,
decisions made,
actions taken,
worldview, and
worship.
Footprints
of some kind of
glory.
May my trail point
others
to the glory
that can only be found in
you.

_____

One generation shall commend your
*   works to another,*
*   and shall declare your mighty acts.*
On the glorious splendor of your
*   majesty,*
*   and on your wonderous works,*
*   I will meditate.*
They shall speak of the might of your
*   awesome deeds,*
*   and I will declare your greatness.*
*   (Ps. 145:4-6)*

What sort of legacy are you leaving
for your friends and family?

What might you do to make your
legacy point toward the glory that can
only be found in God?

For further study and encouragement,
read 1 Corinthians 3:10-15.

Revelation

No
tea-leaf lifestyle of
trying to read the indicators,
hoping to exegete
the past
and divine
the future.

No
hope-for-the-best, or
blind leaps of faith.

No
gotta good feeling, or
saw the light.

No
inner peace
because God told me.
Don't need a
fortune teller.

No
crystal-ball
guidance here.

I need revelation
inspired,
written,
faithful,
practical,
wise,
and true,
with a shelf life
for the ages.

I need something to bank on,
something
I can be sure of.
I need your
revelation.
I need a slow walk
through the wise pages of
your Word.

———

Every word of God proves true;
    he is a shield to those who take
        refuge in him. (Prov. 30:5)

Are you ever tempted to bank on
things other than God's word? Why
might this be?

How can you ensure you devote time
for a "slow walk through the wise
pages" God's word?

For futher study and encouragement,
read 1 Peter 1:13–25.

Saving Grace

Never at stake,
never at risk,
never up for grabs,
never failing,
ever-present,
ever-giving,
infinite,
inexhaustible,
tireless,
faithful,
dependable,
trustworthy,
providing,
protecting,
guiding,
transforming,
rescuing,
delivering,
powerful,
wise,
loving,
patient,
comforting,
confronting,
correcting,
tender,
kind,
gentle,
never impatient,
never disgusted,
never irritated,
never condemning,
always forgiving,
always reconciling,
always restoring,
redeeming,
saving
grace.

_____

For the grace of God has appeared,
bringing salvation for all people.
(Titus 2:11)

Spend some time developing your
own list of words that describe God's
saving grace.

Consider spending time in prayer,
praising God for his saving grace
(and use this poem or your own list
while you pray).

For further study and encouragement,
read John 19.

Afraid

In this fallen world,
diseased,
shattered,
broken,
groaning,
evil,
and dark,
there are many things
to make me
afraid.
Afraid of weakness,
afraid of temptation,
afraid of others,
afraid of the past,
afraid of the future,
afraid of myself,
afraid of sickness,
afraid of sin within,
afraid of evil without,
afraid of being afraid . . .
But in the midst of fear,
I have learned that it is only
fear
that has the power to decimate
fear.
It is only when my
heart
is captured by
fear of you,
that I live with
confidence
and I am no longer
afraid.

‗‗‗‗

The fear of man lays a snare,
*   but whoever trusts in the Lord is*
*   safe. (Prov. 29:25)*

What are some things that cause you
to fear?

How do you think that "fear of the
Lord" would cause all other fears to
lessen?

For further study and encouragement,
read Psalm 2.

Theology

The theology of Scripture
isn't an open invitation to
religious intellectualism
but an opening of long-secret,
divine mysteries
to engender human
belief and personal
transformation.

The theology of Scripture
isn't an esoteric outline
but shorthand for a long-planned,
redemptive narrative.

The theology of Scripture
isn't a philosophical system
but a long-unfolding welcome to
put the trust of your heart
in God.

The theology of Scripture
isn't an answer to every question
but a repeatedly given
invitation
to root the hope of your soul
in the one who is
the answer.

The theology of Scripture
isn't antiseptic and cosmetic
but has the dirt of the long-traveled
streets
of everyday life on it.

The theology of Scripture
isn't about religious
information
but about the grace of
rescue
and the hope and glory of
sanctification.

The theology of Scripture
isn't intended to stand
alone
but is God's graciously given
explanation
of his redeeming plan.

The theology of Scripture
isn't a guide to human
glory
but a call to surrender
all that you are and
have
to the all-surpassing glory of
God.

The theology of Scripture
doesn't have as its final
aim
to inform you
but to rescue you from
you.

The theology of Scripture is
God's welcome
to place your trust in the
only one
who has the power and willingness to
redeem.

_____

The saying is trustworthy and deserving of full acceptance, that
Christ Jesus came into the world to save sinners. (1 Tim. 1:15)

How do you generally view theology? Does this poem change
your opinion at all?

How do theology and the gospel connect?

For further study and encouragement, read 1 Corinthians
3:18–23 and Galatians 1:11–24.

Romans 7

I am a mass of contradictions;
I don't want to be, but I am.
I preach a gospel of peace,
but my life isn't always driven by
    peace.
I talk about a Jesus who alone can
    fully satisfy the soul,
but I am often not satisfied.
I celebrate a theology of amazing
    grace,
but I often react in ungrace.
And if I rest in God's control,
why do I seek it for myself?
Even in moments when I think I am
    prepared,
I end up doing what I didn't want to do.
Irritation,
impatience,
envy,
discontent,
wrong talk,
anger, and
self-focus
are not the fruit of the new life,
are not the way of grace.
So there is this law operating inside
    of me.
When I step out with a desire to do
    good,
evil follows me wherever I go.
There is this war that rages inside
    of me,
between a desire for good and sin.
There are times when I feel like a
    prisoner,
held against my will.
I didn't plan to be mad in the grocery
    store,
but that guy made me mad.
I didn't plan to be discontent,
but it just enveloped me in the
    quietness of the car.
That discussion wasn't supposed to
    degenerate into an argument,
but it did.
I am thankful for God's grace,
but there is daily evidence that I'm
    still in need of help.
That battle inside me cannot be
    solved by
theology,
strategies,
principles,
techniques,
plans,
preparation,
helpful hints, or
outlines.
I have been humbled by the war
I cannot win.
I have been grieved by desires
I cannot conquer.
I have been confronted by actions
I cannot excuse.

And I have come to confess that what
  I really need is
rescue.
So, have mercy on me, oh God,
according to your unfailing love;
according to your great compassion,
blot out my
transgressions.
Wash away all my
iniquity.
And cleanse me from my
sin.
For I know my transgressions,
and my sin is always before me.
I embrace the rescue that could only
  be found
in you.
Thanks be to God
through Jesus Christ our Lord!

For I know my transgressions,
  and my sin is ever before me.
    (Ps. 51:3)

Do you ever feel like a mass of
contraditctions because of the war
inside of you?

What is the way to respond once
you've sinned?

For further study and encouragement,
read Romans 7.

Uber Music

While the minor-key music
of the fallen world
drones on,
sung by the choir
of the lost,
the blind,
the deceived,
the wounded,
the poor,
the weak,

the rebel,
the lame,
the willful,
and the enslaved,
singing the sad notes
of a world
once beautiful,
now broken,
of hearts
once pure,

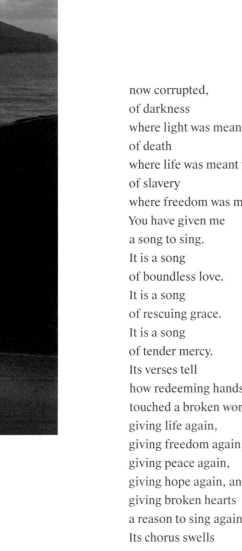

now corrupted,
of darkness
where light was meant to be,
of death
where life was meant to flourish,
of slavery
where freedom was meant to reign.
You have given me
a song to sing.
It is a song
of boundless love.
It is a song
of rescuing grace.
It is a song
of tender mercy.
Its verses tell
how redeeming hands
touched a broken world,
giving life again,
giving freedom again,
giving peace again,
giving hope again, and
giving broken hearts
a reason to sing again.
Its chorus swells
to heights never before sung,
and its constant refrain
is
"Alleluia,
Alleluia to the Lamb,
Alleluia."
Your grace
has placed in my mouth
the only song worth singing.

Your love
has placed on my tongue
the only words worth repeating.
Your mercy
has returned to my heart
the only music worth playing.
It is the song of songs,
and one million years
into eternity
it will be
as beautiful and new
as the moment
the first note was sung.

———

Worthy is the Lamb who was slain,
to receive power and wealth and
    wisdom and might
and honor and glory and blessing!
        (Rev. 5:12)

Does imagining the gospel message
as a song give new insight for you
into the Great Commission?

Consider how and with whom you
might be able to share this "song"
today or in the near future.

For further study and encouragement,
read Revelation 7:9–17.

By Myself

Sitting by myself,
thoughts swallow
internal accounting of
choices,
desires,
actions,
decisions,
words,
and feelings
again falling short.
Righteous standards
out of reach again.
Good intentions
give way to temptation.
Worldly desires
erode vertical love.
Creation resides
on the Creator's throne.
Sin's deception
hides idol cravings.
Accepted from above
yet war down below.
Trangression's struggle
makes Jesus shine clearer.
Invaded darkness
because there was no other way.
Failure preaches
the essentiality of grace.
Boundaries broken
scream for his righteousness.
Life and death struggle
point to a resurrection.

Sitting alone,
but not alone,
his Spirit indwelling,
his righteousness my covering,
his sacrifice justifying,
his grace enabling,
his hope motivating.
Father, Son, and Spirit working,
a fresh start granted—
I rise.

———

And he took a cup, and when he had
given thanks he gave it to them, saying
"Drink of it, all of you, for this is my
blood of the covenant, which is poured
out for many for the forgiveness
of sins." (Matt. 26:27–28)

When by yourself, do you tend to
slip into remembering times you
fell short? If so, do your thoughts
eventually turn to Jesus and his work
done on your behalf?

How can you humbly transform your
mistakes into platforms to display
Christ's glory?

For further study and encouragement,
read 2 Corinthians 5.

Psalm 73 (*Remix*)

Yes, God is good,
but I still stumble.
Sometimes it's hard for me to handle
the fact
that the bad guys seem to keep
winning,
while the good guys seem to have it
so hard.
Sometimes I get caught up in
envying
people I should not envy.
They seem to get away with
murder,
while they flaunt their
disobedience
and mock those who believe
in you.
Meanwhile their success and affluence seem
to increase.
There are moments of weakness when I'm tempted
to listen
to lies that make me wonder if it's been worth it
to obey.
When I am weak and weary,
I am vulnerable.
But it is when I come into
your presence—
in heartfelt worship and remember you
and view my life and their lives from
eternity—
that I remember
they walk in slippery places,

their glory fades like a dream,
and without you they head for
ruin.
Then I remember
you always hold my hand,
you always guide and counsel me,
and you will receive me into glory.
I have no one in heaven
but you.
There's nothing on earth that compares
to you.
When my body is weak and my
heart fails,
you are my heart's strength,
my eternal portion.
It is so good to be
near you.
It is so good that you are my
refuge.

———

My flesh and my heart may fail,
    but God is the strength of my heart and my portion forever.
        (Ps. 73:26)

Have you been annoyed by evil seeming to flourish while good
seems trampled? Consider sharing your frustration with God in
prayer.

Recall times when God has been a refuge for you during hardship.

For further study and encouragement, read Psalm 73.

Why I Hate to Wait

I hate to wait.
I have places to go;
I have people to see;
I have things to do.
I love me
and I have a wonderful plan
for my life.

I hate to wait.
I don't like obstacles
in my way,
people that disagree,
or processes that take too long.

I hate to wait.
I don't like lines,
or traffic,
or delayed appointments,
or tardy people.

I hate to wait.
I wake up every day
with an agenda.
I know
what I want to accomplish.
I know
how I want it done.
I know
where I want it done.
I know
when I want it done.
I know
who I want to do it.

I know
why it has to be done this way.

I hate to wait,
because
I am the one having to wait.
I don't mind
that you have to wait
but I don't want to have to
wait with you.

I hate to wait,
because
I tend to put myself
in the one place
I am never supposed to be
and
I tend to want to be
the one thing
I should never crave to be.

I hate to wait,
because
I want to be
in the center of my universe
and I want to be
my own sovereign.
When I forget your plan,
when I lose sight of your will,
when I begin to think
that my life belongs to me,
when I fall prey to
the delusion

that I am wiser than you
and
my way is better than yours,
then I hate to wait
and
I curse the obstacles in my way.

But you are sovereign
and you are
good,
and loving,
and gracious,
and kind,
and mighty,
and filled with compassion,
and overflowing with mercy.
You bought me
with the price of your Son.
You forgave me,
and the cost was his death.
For all my attempts
at independent wisdom
and
self-sovereignty,
the truth is
that my life does not belong to me.
So
once more I fall to my knees.
Once more I open my hands
and
give my life back to you
and say
"You do with, in, and through me

what you think is best
and
I will follow;
and when
your wisdom and grace
require it,
I will be willing
to wait."

———

Wait for the Lord and keep his way,
and he will exalt you to inherit the
land;
you will look on when the wicked
are cut off. (Ps. 37:34).

Do you hate to wait? What might be
the root cause for such a distaste for
waiting?

Recall times when your waiting was
rewarded.

For further study and encouragement,
read 1 Samuel 13.

Family Forever

I deserve to be
forsaken,
to be forever cast away.
I deserve to be
rejected,
to have you turn away and stay.
I have debated your goodness.
I have questioned your law.
I have doubted your wisdom.
I have run from your love.
I deserve your
anger,
the punishment for my wrong.
I deserve your
righteous judgment,
the full weight of your law.
I have wanted what I wanted.
I have walked from your grace.
I have trespassed your boundaries.
I have envied your throne.
I don't deserve your
affection,
the many things I could not earn.
I don't deserve your
provision,
the daily gifts of your love.
I don't deserve the rights of
family,
to be called your son.
I don't deserve the warm
reception,
tender care, and endless help.

I don't deserve to call you
"Father,"
to be welcomed in your home.
You came to be
rejected,
to have the Father turn his face.
Your bond of family was
broken;
you came to stand in my place.
You didn't deserve to be
rejected,
you came because of your love.
You didn't deserve to be
forsaken,
yet you were willing to the end.

So, now I have a
family,
forever I've been received.
I am never
forsaken,
even when I'm all alone.
When fatherless and
friendless,
you are with me even then.
I have been given a
family
I did not deserve or earn.
The Lord has
received me.
I will never be alone.
Once more I will forsake you.

I will question your love.
Once more I will debate you.
I will turn from your face.
But you will come as a
Father.
You will treat me as a son.
You will forgive and
restore me
with great patience and great love.
In you, I have found a
family.
In you, I have found grace.
And what I've found, I've found
forever.
Forever Father.
Forever family.
Forever welcomed.
Forever loved.

———

For you did not receive the spirit of slavery to fall back into fear, but you have received the Spirit of adoption as sons, by whom we cry, "Abba! Father!" (Rom. 8:15)

Do you find it easy or difficult to imagine that you've been adopted into God's family as an heir? Why might that be?

Have you developed close, family-like relationships with people at your local church? What steps could you take to further cultivate such relationships?

For further study and encouragement, read 1 Peter 2:1–12.

Safe

I am safe,
not because I have no
trouble,
or because I never experience
danger.
I am safe,
not because people affirm
me,
or my plans always
work out.
I am safe,
not because I am immune from
disease,
or free of the potential for
poverty.
I am safe,
not because I am protected from
disappointment,
or separated from this
fallen world.
I am safe,
not because I am
wise
or strong.
I am safe,
not because I deserve
comfort or have earned my
ease.
I am safe,
not because of
money,
or power,
or position,
or intellect,
or who I know,
or where I live.
I am safe because of the glorious
    mystery of
grace.
I am safe because of the presence of
boundless love.
I am safe because of
divine mercy,
divine wisdom,
divine power,
and divine grace.
I am safe,
not because I never face
danger,
but because you are
with me in it.
You have not given me
a ticket out of danger.
You have not promised me
a life of ease.
You have chosen to place me in
a fallen world.
I am safe
because you have given me
the one thing
that is the
only thing
that will ever keep me safe.
You have given me
you.

I am safe
from my evil heart
and this shattered world,
not because I can escape
them both,
but because in the middle of
temptation and trial,
danger and disappointment,
sickness and want,
you give me everything
I need to
fight temptation
and avoid defeat
and to point others
to the safety
that can only be found
in you.
So, I will wake up tomorrow
and face the anxiety
of not knowing,
the fear of my own weakness,
and the reality of the fall.
I will live with
faith,
courage,
perseverance,
and hope.
And when danger comes,
and it will,
I'll whisper to
my weakening heart,
"Emmanuel is your shelter;
you are safe."

———

The name of the Lord is a strong
    tower;
  the righteous man runs into it and
    is safe. (Prov. 18:10)

What are things that make you
feel safe? Consider how the safety
provided by the Lord is better than
these.

How is the safety promised by God
not necessarily comfortable?

For further study and encouragement,
read Joshua 1.

Me and Mine

Privacy fence,
no sidewalks,
attached garage,
personal entertainment center,
frenetic schedule,
half-acre plot.
Individualized living,
a lie of autonomy,
deceit of self-sufficiency,
and a delusion of self-righteousness.
Buy your way out of
need.
Amuse your way out of
reality.
Never known,
never knowing,
never stepping beyond what is
comfortable,
pleasurable,
enjoyable,
predictable,
and safe.
Door-closed silence,
a shrunken community
of me and mine.
Thinking I can do
what I was never designed
to do—
live
all by myself.

———

*Take care, brothers, lest there be in
any of you an evil, unbelieving heart,
leading you to fall away from the
living God. But exhort one another
every day, as long as it is called
"today," that none of you may be
hardened by the deceitfulness of sin.
For we have come to share in Christ, if
indeed we hold our original confidence
firm to the end. (Heb. 3:12-14)*

How well do your friends know you?
How well do you know your friends?

How can you intentionally invite
other Christians to walk alongside
you in deeper fellowship?

For further study and encouragement,
read 1 Thessalonians

Set Free

You have set me free
from the power of sin
outside of me and
inside of me.
You have set me free
from the control of
my fickle desires and
my wandering thoughts.
You have set me free
from the power of the enemy.
You have set me free
from the falsehood that held me.
You have set me free
from the prison of my blindness.
You have set me free
from being controlled by
what cannot satisfy.
You have set me free
from punishment and damnation.
You have set me free
from all that would separate me from
your love.
You have set me free
not so I could establish
my own rule.
You have set me free
so I would be enslaved
to you.
You have enslaved me,
because in serving you
I have been set free.

———

*But now that you have been set free
from sin and have become slaves
of God, the fruit you get leads to
sanctification and its end, eternal life.
For the wages of sin is death, but the
free gift of God is eternal life in Christ
Jesus our Lord. (Rom. 6:22–23)*

When you became a Christian, where
did you see immediate changes in
your thoughts, desires, and actions?
Take some time to pray and thank
God for his redeeming work in
your life.

Where do you need to repent from
sin and seek God's forgiveness and
freedom in your life right now?

For further study and encouragement,
read Romans 8.

You Chose

You chose this difficult thing.
You chose this unexpected moment.
You planned this unplanned season.
You decided to lead me into mystery.
You ordained the trial I am now in.
You led me into this valley.
You led me beyond the borders of my understanding,
wisdom,
maturity,
and strength.

You chose this difficult thing.
You chose that it would be a
humbling thing,
a convicting thing,
a transforming thing.
You chose to trouble my normal
    sources of hope
so I would find hope in you.
I do not need to
doubt,
fear,
panic,
hide,
run,
accuse,
or rebel,
because you did not only choose this
    difficult thing,
you chose me.
And because you chose me,

I know you will not abandon me.
You will complete everything for me
you have chosen to do.

———

*And I am sure of this, that he who
began a good work in you will bring
it to completion at the day of Jesus
Christ. (Phil. 1:6)*

In your present circumstances, where
are you confused about God's plan
for your life? Are you worried about
the future?

Do you have confidence in God's
ability to do his good work in and
through you? Where does this
confidence come from, and how can
you build more of it?

For further study and encouragement,
read Hebrews 11.

Eavesdrop on Eternity

Here and now,
so visible,
so powerful,
so compelling.
See,
hear,
taste,
touch,
measure,
quantify,
acquire,
possess,
and serve.
I need
values,
perspective,
direction,
purpose,
and deliverance from
the magnetic draw
of here and now.
I need
my soul corrected,
my desires focused,
my purposes sanctified.
I need to
eavesdrop on eternity.

———

If in Christ we have hope in this life only, we are of all people most to be pitied. (1 Cor. 15:19)

What everyday problems absorb your attention?

Are you so focused on the here and now that you have lost sight of eternity? How can you regularly adjust your perspective?

For further study and encouragement, read 2 Corinthians 4.

Functional Blindness

I would like to think
that others are blind,
but I am not.
I would like to think
that I have
clarity of vision
and penetrating insight
that lights my way.
I am good
at recognizing
the sight problems of others.
I am skilled
at pointing out
the gaps in their vision
and the blind spots
that alter how they
see
and the way they
respond.
I would like to
believe
that I have 20/20 vision,
but the evidence points
to the sad fact that
I don't.
I have the stunning ability
to look around
and not see you.
I see my
busy schedule with
tasks to complete,
problems to solve,
people to see,
demands to meet,
things to repair,
pressures to face,
temptations to fight,
pleasures to consume,
things to build,
things to tear down,
plans to make,
difficulties to survive,
responsibilities to hold,
days to complete.

I gaze at my life
every day
and again and again I fail
to see you.
It is a scary
reality,
humbling to admit.
Though this world
is filled with
your glory,
I exist
so much of the time
glory blind.
In your love,
you created a world
that is a sight and sound
display
of your magnificent
glory.
No matter from what perspective
we're looking,
no matter what vista
we're taking in,

no matter
where we're standing
and which way
we're gazing—
your glory is visible
and evident.
Yet, again and again
I fail to see
your beauty.
So, I seek your
healing
one more time.
Please, place your
powerful hands
on my broken eyes
and give me sight again.
Please place your
powerful hands
on my wayward heart
and make it seek you again.
Don't let me be
so blinded
with me and mine,

that I fail to see
you.
For it's only
when my eyes
see your
beauty,
and my heart
is filled with your
glory,
that I'll quit seeking
identity,
meaning,
satisfaction,
purpose,
fulfillment,
and life
where they can't be found.
So, I would pray
this simple prayer:
"Please touch me by
your grace
so that there'll never
be a day
where I haven't
somehow,
some way
gazed upon
your beauty."

_____

One thing have I asked of the LORD,
that will I seek after:
that I may dwell in the house of the
LORD
all the days of my life,
to gaze upon the beauty of the LORD
and to inquire in his temple.
(Ps. 27:4)

What everyday temptations and sins
contribute to your spiritual blindness?

In your work, schedule, and routine,
whose kingdom are you building:
yours or God's? How can you seek
and build God's kingdom in your
everyday life?

For further study and encouragement,
read Mark 4.

My Calling

Brief moments of
kingdom-consciousness
followed by
days and days
of self-sovereignty
and self-interest.
I give so little of me,
yet I have received
so much of you.
I treat ministry
like a big,
giant step
out of what is mine
into
what is yours.
Yet,
there is no
mine and yours.
You have
purchased me
with your blood.
All that I have
and
all that I am
belongs to you
for your keeping,
for your using,
for your kingdom,
for your glory.
All that I am,
wherever I am,
whatever the time,
will be used in service of you.

This is my calling;
this is your will.

———

I appeal to you therefore, brothers,
by the mercies of God, to present
your bodies as a living sacrifice, holy
and acceptable to God, which is your
spiritual worship. (Rom. 12:1)

Do you consider a "calling" some-
thing God only provides for pastors
or clergy? How has God called you to
where you are today?

Do you consider ministry something
that only happens in a church
building, with church people, or in
designated church activities? How
can you view your work, marriage,
parenting, friendships, and everyday
life as ministry?

For further study and encouragement,
read 2 Timothy 1.

The Swindle

No one swindles me more than
I do.
I have a perverse ability
to cause myself to feel good
about what you say is not good.
I fail to stop the desires
I should resist.
I fail to let my theology
guide my living.
I speak in ways that fail to
give grace.
I demand my way at the exclusion of
your way.
My thoughts are not always pure;
my actions are not always obedient.
Sometimes my heart submits to you;
sometimes it wanders.
Kidnapped by self-love,
I fail to give and serve.
I am able to make myself feel okay
     about
what you say is not okay.
I desperately need what I do not have
on my own.
I need my mind
rescued.
I need my private conversation
interrupted.
I need my heart
chained to you.
I need wisdom that I do not have
on my own.

I need willingness that I do not have
on my own.
I need resolve that I do not have
on my own.
I need power that I do not have
on my own.
I need forgiveness that I cannot gain
on my own.
I cannot live as you designed for me
     to live
on my own.
So I am thankful that,
by grace,
you don't leave me
on my own.

———

And lead us not into temptation,
*   but deliver us from evil.*
*   (Matt. 6:13)*

What creative excuses are you
tempted to believe about your sin?

When you sin, are you tempted to run
to or *from* God? When you sin, what
do you need most? Where can you
find it?

For further study and encouragement,
read Genesis 3.

Salt and Fire

It would have been a tasteless life
without the salt of your grace,
an inedible existence
were it not seasoned by your mercy.
It would have been raw and undone
if not for the fires of your conviction.
I was not meant to savor life—
to taste its elements,
to chew and swallow,
to find satisfaction and pleasure,
to crave for more,
to consume again and again—
until my life has
every single ingredient.
All that makes me—
every thought and intention,
every quest and craving,
every purpose and motivation,
every recess and secret—
has been touched,
altered,
made new by your deft, redemptive
    hand.
With all that I could muster,
I could never have hoped to do
what the salt and fire of redemption
has miraculously done
for me,
in me.
Now may I be your vessel

through which you do for others
what you have done
for me.
And may I always remember
what I was,
what I couldn't be,
what I couldn't do,
and what I needed from you.
So when I am tempted to speak of me,
I instead speak of you
and celebrate once again
what the salt and fire of your
mercy
has miraculously done
for me,
in me.
Now may I be your vessel
through which you do for others
what you have done
for me.
And may I always remember
what I was,
what I couldn't be,
what I couldn't do,
what I needed from you,
so that if I am tempted to feed on other
    food,
I will run to your table, and
I will feed on you.

——

For everyone will be salted with fire. Salt is good, but if the salt has lost its saltiness, how will you make it salty again? Have salt in yourselves, and be at peace with one another. (Mark 9:49–50)

How has grace seasoned your life like salt? How have trials refined your life like fire?

How easily satisfied are you with little bits of Bible? How can you learn to hunger more for God and feed more upon Christ?

For further study and encouragement, read Malachi 3.

Good and Angry

It's an everyday
experience,
a bit of an embarrassment.
It is more of a theme
than I would care to
admit.
It's revealed in moments of
low-grade irritation,
grumbling impatience,
turnstile complaints,
argumentative responses,
dissatisfied looks.
I am angry;
no, not because
my world is broken;
no, not because
injustice exists;
no, not because
war and violence destroy lives and
   communities;
no, not because
falsehood gets a wider hearing than
   truth;
no, not because
of the suffering that is all around me.
No,
I am angry because
I want to be in control.
I am angry because
people and things
get in my way.
So, I cry out for your help.

I seek your rescue,
not that I would be anger-free,
but that I would be
good
and
angry
at the same time.

————

Know this, my beloved brothers:
let every person be quick to hear,
slow to speak, slow to anger; for the
anger of man does not produce the
righteousness of God. (James 1:19–20)

What makes you angry?

Do you get angry when your kingdom
has been interrupted, or when God's
kingdom has been offended?

For further study and encouragement,
read Psalm 7.

Joy

All of the
shiny,
sparkling,
attractive,
glimmering,
luminescent,
seductive
baubles of the material world
have no power to do for me what
I want them to do.
I see them,
I crave them,
I seek them,
I plan for them,
I acquire them,
but when brought into my life,
when held in my hands,
when embraced by my heart,
they fail me.
They cannot provide for me the
joy
I never stop seeking.
No material thing can produce
joy.
Nothing I can hold in my hands can bring
joy
to my longing heart.
Nothing I've paid for will give me
joy.
The rush of temporary excitement,
the buzz of a new possession,
the power of acquisition, and

the enjoyment of using
should not be confused with
joy.
Material pleasure for as long as
it lasts
may masquerade as
joy,
but it is not
joy.
The DNA of joy is
gratitude.
In the center of gratitude lives
contentment.
Contentment is being willing to live
 inside the
boundaries
of what God has provided, and
joy
is recognizing
the person providing,
the riches provided,
the grace of provision,
the faithfulness depicted,
and the love behind it all.
Joy and contentment
celebrate
what is.
Discontentment
meditates on what could be.
May I have the
grace
to see your providing hand,

to love the giver more than the
gift,
and may the worship of my heart
produce what created things can't—
lasting,
robust,
contented,
sturdy,
vertical,
internal
joy.

———

*Keep your life free from love of money,
and be content with what you have, for
[God] has said, "I will never leave you
nor forsake you." (Heb. 13:5)*

Think about a time when a purchase
or gift made you happy. How long
did that feeling last? What purchase
are you currently thinking about,
planning for, and excited about?

How can you build contentment in
your life?

For further study and encouragement,
read 1 Timothy 6.

Rescue the Perishing

I was not designed
to be on my own,
to author my own story,
to compose my own rules,
to live with me in the center.

I was not designed
to look for life outside of you;
to treasure the creation,
to love people, places, and things
more than you.

I was not designed
to rely on my wisdom,
to trust my imagination,
to rely on my thoughts,
to ignore your revelation.

I was not designed
to follow the paths of my craving;
to be enslaved to my desires,
to be ruled by my passions
more than I am by you.

I was not designed
to put created things in your place,
to look to the creation
to fulfill the longings
that only you can fulfill.

I was not designed
to live for the moment,
to ignore what is forever,
to covet what belongs to others,
forgetting I've been given you.

I was not designed
to question your goodness,
to bring you to the court of my judgment,
to be bitter in my assessment
of the things you do.

I was not designed
to let my heart fill with envy,
to be constantly accounting,
to be jealous and untrusting
instead of resting in you.

I was not designed
to disregard your right hand that
    holds me,
to ignore your good counsel that
    teaches me,
to neglect your presence that supports me,
or to forget your promise of eternity
    with you.

I was not designed
to think that I am living,
to ignore the evidence that I'm dying,
to forget that we all perish
when separate from you.

So I acknowledge this morning
that it is good to be with you,
that you are my sole refuge,
that I will speak daily of your workings.
Whom do I have but you?
I praise you for rescuing me,
for holding me near you,

for owning my heart's desires,
for teaching me that
my life is you.

——

Whom have I in heaven but you?
    And there is nothing on earth that I
        desire besides you.
My flesh and my heart may fail,
    but God is the strength of my
        heart and my portion forever.
    (Ps. 73:25–26)

Do you love yourself and have a
wonderful plan for your life?
How do you respond when "your will" is
not done?

How can you live beyond your
own glory and your own kingdom?
How can you better practice what you
believe, that Christ is the center of
your life?

For further study and encouragement,
read Psalm 121.

The Quest

It's the quest everyone
seeks.
It's the question everyone
asks.
It's the drama everyone
plays.
> *Who am I?*
> *What is my value?*
> *Where do I find it?*
> *What does it all mean?*
> *What is my purpose?*
> *Where will I find it?*
> *Why am I here?*

Sadly, for so many, the quest
never ends,
and the questions are
never answered.
Most people look for
answers

where answers won't be
found.
They look for meaning
in meaningless places.
They look for identity
where no identity is formed.
It is the grand mistake
of the lost and weary
to look horizontally
for what will only ever be found
vertically.
The quest is more than a quest for
identity,
or meaning,
or purpose,
or value.
The quest of quests
is not for a thing,
not for an idea.

No.
It's a lifelong quest for
you.
Blind eyes are confronted by
you,
but blind eyes don't see
you.
The quest only ends
when grace gives
sight
to see the unseen
and hearts are given faith to
believe.
The quest ends with a
miracle,
but it's not the miracle of
identity found.
No, it's the miracle of
redemption accomplished.

———

But may all who seek you
    rejoice and be glad in you;
may those who love your salvation
    say continually, "Great is the
        Lord!" (Ps. 40:16)*

How does sin cause you to look
horizontally for meaning, purpose,
and value?

How is your meaning, purpose, and
value changed when you look verti-
cally? What daily spiritual disciplines
help you look and live vertically?

For further study and encouragement,
read Colossians 1.

Hoping for a Broken Heart

I am too satisfied
with the things I say,
the things I do,
the attitudes of my heart,
the ways I react
day
after
day
after
day.
I too easily
accept
quick assessments
of my own righteousness
in situations
where I have been
anything but
righteous.
I am too skilled
at mounting

plausible arguments
structured
to make me feel okay
about what I think,
what I desire,
what I say,
what I do.
I am too defensive
when a loved one
makes an attempt
to call me out
and suggests
for a moment
that what I
have decided,
said,
or done
is less than
godly.
I am too

comfortable
with the state of things
between
you and me,
too relaxed
with the nature
of my love for you,
too able to
minimize
my need for your
grace.
In the recesses
of my private
world,
there is so much
that is wrong
that I am able
to convince myself
is right.
There are attitudes
that should not be kept.
There are words
that should not be spoken.
There are thoughts
that do not agree
with your view
of me
and mine.
There are desires
that take me in a
different direction
than what you have planned
for me.
I make decisions
based more on what
I want
than on what
you will.

So I am hoping
for
wise eyes
that are able
to see through
the cloud of
self-righteousness
and see myself
as I actually
am.

I am praying
for
wise ears
that are able
to hear through
the background noise of
well-used platitudes
and hear myself
with clarity.
And I am longing

for
a humble spirit
that is willing
to
accept and confess
what you reveal
as you break through
my defenses
and show me
to me.
I am hoping
for
a broken heart.

———

O Lord, open my lips,
    and my mouth will declare your
      praise.
For you will not delight in sacrifice, or
    I would give it;
    you will not be pleased with a burnt
      offering.
The sacrifices of God are a broken
      spirit;
    a broken and contrite heart, O
      God, you will not despise.
    (Ps. 51:15–17)

How are you "too satisfied" with your Christian life? Consider areas such as your Bible reading, prayer, ministry, besetting sins, and spiritual growth.

Do you have other Christians in your life who can speak honestly to you? How do you respond when they help you see your sin?

For further study and encouragement, read 1 Peter 2.

Time

We think so much of
moments,
days,
years,
times past,
and things to come.
We deal with so much
regret of the past,
fear of the future,
and confusion in the present.
For us
time passes quickly—
we miss a moment;
or time creeps slowly—
days drag on.
We
anticipate what's coming
and hold on to what's gone.
Time
holds us,
molds us,
controls us.
Thankfully
God knows no time,
never expects,
never regrets—
no looking forward,
no glancing back,
no surprises,
no mysteries,
nothing unexpected.
God dwells in an
eternal now.
All that he is,

he has forever been
and will forever be.
With him there is no
growth,
change,
or becoming.
He is security's foundation,
time's sovereign.
In a world where
everything is
ever-changing,
he is a rock of
secure,
unchanging,
eternal hope.

———

Jesus Christ is the same yesterday and today and forever. (Heb. 13:8)

What do you dwell on in your past? What do you worry about in your future?

Do you listen more to your anxious thoughts or to God's eternal promises?
How can you meditate today on God's unchanging love for you?

The Holy of Holies

In the holy of holies,
my deepest thoughts dwell.
In the secret place
of the heart,
no one sees,
and no one knows.
In that place, worship
sets the course
for all I say
and all I do.

In the holy of holies,
thoughts afraid to be verbal
and desires never quite spoken
determine

what I will seek,
and say,
and do.

In the holy of holies,
greed lurks dark,
and anger stands dangerous.
In the shadows,
lust captivates,
and envy enslaves.
In that sacred place
of the heart,
I plan what I will do
and rehearse what I will say.

In the holy of holies,
love is born
or succumbs to hate,
and gentleness
falls to vengeance.
In that place,
thinking never ends,
and interpretations
become a way of seeing.

In the holy of holies,
feelings grow in power
and overwhelm
what is sensible,
good,
and true.

In the holy of holies,
I stand naked,
before you,
all covering gone.
What I am,
as I am,
void of defense,
stripped of excuse,
with nowhere to hide
and no reputation to polish.

In the holy of holies,
you
can see,
and hear,
and know.
May you do there
what I cannot do.

May you create there
what only mercy can give.
May you hold back
what I deserve
and give what
I could never earn.
May you create in me
a clean heart.

_____

Create in me a clean heart, O God,
  and renew a right spirit within me.
Cast me not away from your presence,
  and take not your Holy Spirit
    from me.
Restore to me the joy of your salvation,
  and uphold me with a willing
    spirit. (Ps. 51:10–12)

How do you want others to see
you? What do you regularly use to
piece together your identity: your
accomplishments, your stuff, your
relationships, or your social media
highlights?

Who knows and sees everything
about you? Who loves you
unconditionally?

For further study and encouragement,
read Psalm 139.

Goodness

I have one place of confidence,
one place of rest,
one place of peace,
and one place of hope.
I have one place of surety,
where courage
can be found
and strength
waits for the taking.
I have one place of wisdom
where foolishness wanes
and truth grants freedom.
Alone I am not confident;
I have no pride in my strength,
or knowledge,
or character.
I know
who I am,
the duplicity of my heart,
the weakness of my resolve,
and the covert disloyalty
that make me susceptible
to temptation's hook.
I have one place of confidence—
it isn't a theology,
a book,
a set of principles,
a well-researched observation,
or a worldview.
No, my confidence is in you.
You are my hope because
you are good.

I rest in the goodness
of your sovereignty,
in the goodness
of your power,
in the goodness
of your faithfulness,
in the goodness
of your wisdom,
in the goodness
of your patience,
in the goodness
of your mercy,
in the goodness
of your holiness,
and in the goodness
of your grace.
I have learned
(and I am learning)
that the physical delights
of the created world
were not designed to be
the source
and hope
of my confidence.
No, all of those things
in their temporary elegance
were meant to be
signposts
that point me to the
eternal,
never-failing,
ever-available,

never-changing,
ever-holy,
grace-infused
goodness that can only be found
in you.
I have learned
(and I am learning)
that confident living
always rests its foundation
on you.
I am confident
because of this solitary thing—
you are,
and you are good.

———

I believe that I shall look upon the
    goodness of the LORD
    in the land of the living!
Wait for the LORD;
    be strong, and let your heart take
        courage;
    wait for the LORD! (Ps. 27:13–14)

In your life and ministry, what gives
you confidence: your theology,
self-control, self-discipline, work
ethic, or personal morality?

Do you spend more time reflecting
on your own behavior or on God's
goodness? Where can you find true
confidence?

For further study and encouragement,
read Ephesians 1.

Under Attack

Under attack again.
Such is life
in a broken world
where sin still
lives,
where the enemy still
lurks,
where broken
things
and broken
people
do not do the things
they were made to do.
Under attack again.
Why was I surprised?
Why did I give way
to anger,
to fear,
to discouragement,
to vengeance,
and to questioning
the one thing that is
sure,
safe,
constant,
and reliable?
You have promised
to keep me,
to protect me,
to nurture me,
to love me,
to defend me,

to defeat my foes.
I have rested
in the hollow of your hand.
I have hidden
under the shelter of your wing.
I have had your peace
put me to sleep.
I have had your presence
comfort my heart.
I have had your Spirit
give me new strength.
Yet somehow,
when under attack again,
I forgot you,
and in forgetting,
I did what I
regret;
I said what gives me
grief;
I questioned
you.
The enemies I face
are too great.
The brokenness around me
is too pervasive.
The sin inside of me
I cannot escape.
So I have come home again,
home to the one thing
I daily need
in moments
mundane and great—

the rescue that only
can be found
in you.
I know that in the face of
your wisdom,
your control,
your power,
and your righteousness,
the enemies of my soul
will stumble,
will fall,
and will crumble in defeat.
When evil comes
(and it will),
I will
remember you,
run to you,
believe in you,
rest in you,
and, with
hands that are clean
and a
heart that is pure,
I will fight evil,
not with words
of evil
or actions
of vengeance,
but with the one thing
the enemy cannot defeat—
worship of you.

———

*One thing have I asked of the L*ORD*,*
    that will I seek after:
that I may dwell in the house of the
    *L*ORD
     all the days of my life,
*to gaze upon the beauty of the L*ORD
    and to inquire in his temple.
       (Ps. 27:4)

What is your "one" thing, the thing
that will make you happy or give you
peace? Where is the one place you
will find true safety and strength?

In your daily battle against sin, where
do you look for safety and strength?
Think about the ways you seek power,
control, approval, or comfort.

For further study and encouragement,
read Psalm 61.

Wait and War

Joy crashes into
sorrow.
Strength collides with
weakness.
Despair washes over
hope.
Pain slices into
peace.
Longing overwhelms
contentment.
Hatred stains the fabric of
love.
Reconciliation wars with
prejudice.
Entitlement weakens
service.
Sin pulls against
righteousness.
Division leaves fissures in
unity.
Idols capture
worship.
Light battles with
darkness.

Impatience cripples
perseverance.
Autonomy grapples with
surrender.
Lies work to silence
truth.
Such is life between
"the already" and "the not yet."
Such is the journey in a world that is
groaning.
So we wait and we
war,
but we do not wait or war
alone
because the Great Victor is
with us,
in us,
and for us.
He will have the
final say.
His will
will be
done.

―――――

At the end of the days I, Nebuchadnezzar, lifted my eyes to heaven, and my reason returned to me, and I blessed the Most High, and praised and honored him who lives forever,

> *for his dominion is an everlasting dominion,*
> *and his kingdom endures from generation to generation;*
> *all the inhabitants of the earth are accounted as nothing,*
> *and he does according to his will among the host of heaven and among the inhabitants of the earth;*
> *and none can stay his hand or say to him, "What have you done?" (Dan. 4:34–35)*

What has God *already* done to save you? What has *not yet* happened in God's story of redemption?

Where do you see your life, in the middle of this *already* and *not yet*? Do you sometimes feel alone in your journey?

For further study and encouragement, read Acts 17:22–34.

No More "If Only"

It's so easy to slip into an "if only" lifestyle.
I find myself slipping into it often.
The "if only" possibilities are endless.
If only I'd been from a more stable family . . .
If only I'd had better friends as I was growing up . . .
If only my parents had sent me to better schools . . .
If only I'd been given better intellectual gifts . . .
If only that accident hadn't happened . . .
If only I'd had better physical health . . .
If only that degree program had been as good as advertised . . .
If only I'd been able to find a better job . . .
If only I didn't have to fight the traffic every day . . .
If only I'd been able to get married . . .
If only I hadn't gotten married so young . . .
If only I'd understood marriage more before I got married . . .
If only I had a more understanding spouse . . .
If only I'd come to know Christ earlier . . .
If only I'd found a good church when I was young . . .
If only I didn't have to struggle with my finances . . .
If only it was easier and more comfortable for me to communicate with
    others . . .
If only I could find a small group that I could be comfortable with . . .
If only I could have had children . . .
If only my children were more obedient . . .
If only I knew the Bible better . . .
If only that boss hadn't fired me . . .
If only I had a better place to live . . .
If only I could find some place where I feel like I really belong . . .
If only God seemed closer to me . . .
If only I didn't have to work so hard to make ends meet . . .
If only . . .

———

I know how to be brought low, and I know how to abound. In any and every circumstance, I have learned the secret of facing plenty and hunger, abundance and need. I can do all things through him who strengthens me. (Phil. 4:12-13)

How is an "if only" lifestyle detrimental?

What can you do to avoid slipping into this sort of thought pattern?

For further study and encouragement, read Psalm 37.

The Dance of Redemption

My sin—
your unfailing love.
My transgression—
your great compassion.
My iniquity—
your cleansing.
My evil—
your mercy.
My sin—
your wisdom.
My iniquity—
your presence.
My transgression—
your restoration.
My sin—
your salvation.
My song—
your righteousness.
My broken heart—
your delight.
My prosperity—
your good pleasure.

Your altar—
my delight.
Hide your face
from my sins.
Create in me
a pure heart.
Do not
cast me from your presence.
Do not
take your Spirit from me.
Restore to me
the joy of my salvation.
Grant me
a willing spirit.
Save me
from bloodguilt.
Sustain me.
For I know
my transgressions,
and my sin
is ever before me.

———

You have said, "Seek my face."
  My heart says to you,
"Your face, Lᴏʀᴅ, do I seek."
  Hide not your face from me.
Turn not your servant away in anger,
  O you who have been my help.
Cast me not off; forsake me not,
  O God of my salvation!
  (Ps. 27:8–9)

What do you most often ask God for
when you pray?

Do you more often ask God to
change your *circumstances* or change
your heart? Do you more often ask
God to change your *behavior* or
change your heart?

For further study and encourage-
ment, read Psalm 51.

Life View

I want to view my life through the lens of your
creation artistry.
I want to view my life through the lens of
the parted Red Sea.
I want to view my life through the lens of
the manna in the wilderness.
I want to view my life through the lens of
your promises to Abraham.
I want to view my life through the lens of
the crumbling walls of Jericho.
I want to view my life through the lens of
the defeat of Goliath.
I want to view my life through the lens of
the widow's endless oil.
I want to view my life through the lens of
the survivors of the fiery furnace.
I want to view my life through the lens of
the virgin giving birth.
I want to view my life through the lens of
your manger humility.
I want to view my life through the lens of
the feeding of the multitude.
I want to view my life through the lens of
the resurrected Lazarus.
I want to view my life through the lens of
the glory of the transfiguration.
I want to view my life through the lens of
your cross of suffering.
I want to view my life through the lens of
the empty tomb.
I want to view my life through the lens of
your ascension to glory.

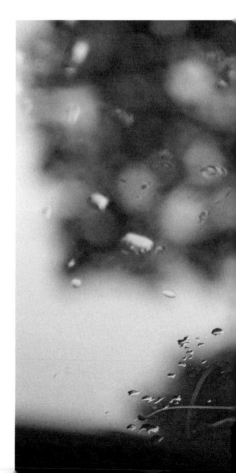

I want to view my life through the lens of
the indwelling Spirit.
I want to view my life through the lens of
your power, presence, and glory.
I want to view my life through the lens of
your love, mercy, and grace.
I want to view my life through the lens of
who you are and who I am in you.
I want to view my life
with wisdom, hope, and courage.
I want to view my life
through you.

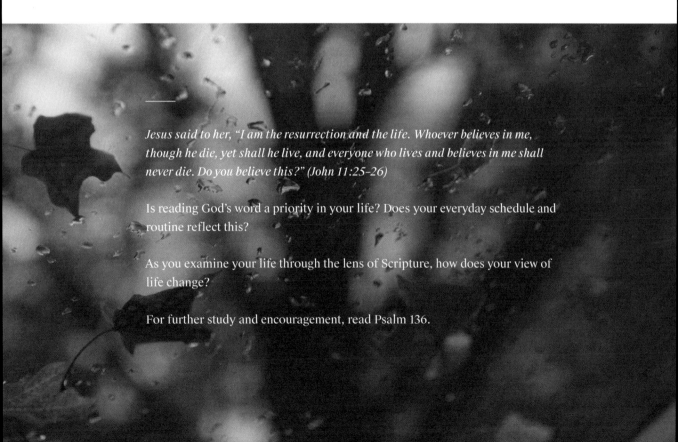

Jesus said to her, "I am the resurrection and the life. Whoever believes in me, though he die, yet shall he live, and everyone who lives and believes in me shall never die. Do you believe this?" (John 11:25–26)

Is reading God's word a priority in your life? Does your everyday schedule and routine reflect this?

As you examine your life through the lens of Scripture, how does your view of life change?

For further study and encouragement, read Psalm 136.

Broken-Down House

Shards of window glass
shimmer
in
weed-strewn sod.
Roof shingles
clap
with the wind,
a spontaneous ovation
for
the dwelling
that once was.
With creaking voices,
dark halls
repeat
long-gone conversations.
Too much
decay,
too much
damage;
violent elements
have disrespected
the carpenter's
dream.
The sagging-porch frown
tells a painful story
of beauty shattered.
All that's left
is a
broken-down house.

———

*For we know that the whole creation
has been groaning together in the
pains of childbirth until now. And not
only the creation, but we ourselves,
who have the firstfruits of the Spirit,
groan inwardly as we wait eagerly for
adoption as sons, the redemption of
our bodies. (Rom. 8:22–23)*

When you see the evidence of sin's
curse in the world, what is your
response? Do you complain about the
world or cry out to God?

Do you long more for short-term
fixes or eternal paradise?

For further study and encouragement,
read John 14.

To Be You

I have a confession to make.
It's something I do in the
        protection of
my home,
in the secret chambers of
my heart.
I know I shouldn't do it,
but I find myself returning to it
again and again.
It's an act of self-will.
It's wanting my own way.
It's about my purpose,
plan,
will,
comfort,
security,
ease,
and contentment.
It resists the life that you've
called me to.
It rebels against the plan
you will for me.
It is selfishness replacing
worship.
It is independence replacing
surrender.
It is self-reliance at war with
faith.
Deep in my heart, in secret moments
        only seen
by you

and only known
by me,
I want all the answers that
you have.
I want your secrets known
to me.
I am weary of surprises.
I don't want to have wonder.
I get exhausted with confusion.
I tire of being unprepared.
I don't want to have to live
by faith.
I don't want to have to rely
on you.
I resist the daily surrender of
        admitting that
I don't have to know what
you know.
My security is in knowing
that you know it all and that
you rule everything I don't know
for your glory
and for my good.
Every day,
somehow, some way, my rest in you
battles
with my desire to know
what you know.
So, once again I cry,
"Lord, I believe;
help my unbelief!"

———

"And it has often cast him into fire and into water, to destroy him. But if you can do anything, have compassion on us and help us." And Jesus said to him, "'If you can'! All things are possible for one who believes." Immediately the father of the child cried out and said, "I believe; help my unbelief!" (Mark 9:22–24)

When you struggle with secret, unconfessed sin, what seems bigger in your mind: your sin, or God's grace?

Do you not like others to see you as spiritually needy? Do you hesitate to ask for help from others or from God? When you ask for help, do you hope for changed behavior or a transformed heart?

For further study and encouragement, read Psalm 51.

Sign Beauty

God has filled his world with beauty.
There is the beauty of:
the delicate orchid,
the spotted leopard,
the multihued sunset,
the pillowy cloud,
the golden sun,
the delicious meal,
the giant oak,
the iridescent snake,
the white-capped wave,
the ribbony grain of wood,
the song of a bird,
the endless variety of music,
the flash of lightning,
the shimmering scales of a fish,
the new, white snow,
the rugged rocks of the mountain,
the tender kiss,
the whisper of the breeze,
the green curtain of the leaves,
the security of a father's voice,
the tender touch of a mother's hand,
the crystal display of a starry night,
the percussive song of a rainy day,
the green of the pasture,
the blue of the sky,
the black of the night,
the brown of the soil,
the yellow of the bee,
the red of the rose,
the white of the cloud.

———

O Lord, our Lord,
  how majestic is your name in all the
    earth!
You have set your glory above the
    heavens.
When I look at your heavens, the work of
    your fingers,
    the moon and the stars, which you
      have set in place,
what is man that you are mindful of him,
    and the son of man that you care for
      him?
Yet you have made him a little lower than
    the heavenly beings
    and crowned him with glory and
      honor.
You have given him dominion over the
    works of your hands;
    you have put all things under his feet,
O Lord, our Lord,
  how majestic is your name in all the
    earth! (Ps. 8:1, 3–6, 9)

Where do you look for beauty?

When you see beauty, do you think
about its source? Are you so captivated
by the created beauty that you miss the
beauty of the Creator?

For further study and encouragement,
read Psalm 104.

You Are Not Like Me

I am good at it—
a skill
I don't think I ever
had to learn.
It resides in my
heart.
It is an anti-social
instinct,
but it shapes my
relationships.
I am able to look at
people
and not see
people.
My craving
heart
reduces them to
vehicles that deliver,
or obstacles in the way of,
what I want.
The only
hope
for me is that
you are not like me.
You are
love,
and you are
delivering
me from me.

———

Having purified your souls by your obedience to the truth for a sincere brotherly love, love one another earnestly from a pure heart, since you have been born again, not of perishable seed but of imperishable, through the living and abiding word of God. (1 Pet. 1:22–23)

When you're focused on yourself, how are you tempted to view others? Do you want people to serve your "kingdom" or God's?

How can you be willing to have your life "complicated" by the needs and struggles of others?

For further study and encouragement, read 1 John 4:7-21.

The Theology of Beauty

Beauty.
What is
beauty?
How is
beauty?
Where is
beauty?
Is beauty without a
beginning?
Is beauty without an
end?
Could it be that there are
only
two kinds of beauty?

In this world there is
source beauty
and
reflected beauty.
Source beauty is
true beauty,
pure beauty,
timeless beauty,
independent beauty,
definitional beauty,
divine beauty.
Reflected beauty is
shadow beauty,
tainted beauty,
dependent beauty,
ill-defined beauty,
creation beauty.

All sin is sin against
beauty.
Idolatry puts
reflected beauty
in
source beauty's place.
Sin hammers reflected
beauty
into the shape of
ugly.
Sin then names ugly
beautiful.
The more distant it is from its
source,

the less beauty there is to be
found
in reflected beauty.
Source beauty is not to be
manipulated
or
ignored.
It is only
ever
eternally to be
worshiped.

In the
incarnation,
the feet of beauty
touched earth
to reveal
beauty,
to teach
beauty,
to restore
beauty,
to help beauty be
seen,
experienced,
worshiped,
and loved
in the hearts of men.
Source beauty
would be restored
to its
rightful place.

But
I still live
in the middle of
a beauty war.
And in the
fog
of the
conflict
I do not see beauty
clearly.
With battle-scarred
eyes
I look at what is
ugly,
and I think I see
beauty.
Please heal
my eyes,
please restore
my heart,
so I may
gaze nowhere else
to
see,
love,
and worship
the beauty
that only
ever
emanates
from you.

The heavens declare the glory of God,
  and the sky above proclaims his handiwork.
Day to day pours out speech,
  and night to night reveals knowledge.
There is no speech, nor are there words,
  whose voice is not heard.
Their voice goes out through all the earth,
  and their words to the end of the world. (Ps. 19:1–4)

What is reflected beauty? What is source beauty? Where are you tempted to be distracted by reflected beauty and blind to source beauty?

What does God's word describe as ugly? How are you tempted to see these ugly things as beautiful?

For further study and encouragement, read Psalm 145.

Light and Darkness

Light and darkness
there in the garden,
Light and darkness
there at the flood,
Light and darkness
there in Egypt,
Light and darkness
there at the Red Sea,
Light and darkness
there at Sinai,
Light and darkness
there in the wilderness,
Light and darkness
there on the shores of the Jordan,
Light and darkness
battle in the Promised Land,
Light and darkness
in kings and judges,
Light and darkness
in the struggle of the prophets,
Light and darkness
at the birth of Jesus,
Light and darkness

in the days of the Messiah,
Light and darkness
in the challenges of the church,
Light and darkness
in the heart of everyone,
Light and darkness
in the great war,
Light and darkness
from beginning to end . . .

The light and darkness battle
will end.
The true light
has come.
The true light
has won an eternal victory.
The true light
has promised to come once again.
The true light
will welcome us to that home
where light will shine without
    darkness
forever.

———

Blessed be the name of God forever and ever,
*   to whom belong wisdom and might.*
He changes times and seasons;
*   he removes kings and sets up kings;*
he gives wisdom to the wise
*   and knowledge to those who have understanding;*
he reveals deep and hidden things;
*   he knows what is in the darkness,*
*   and the light dwells with him. (Dan. 2:20–22)*

Where do you feel the darkness of sin in your life right now?

How does remembering the victory of the true light help you in your
struggles against sin? How can you take time today to meditate on
Jesus, the light of the world?

For further study and encouragement, read John 1.

Listening to Luther

"With Paul, we absolutely deny the possibility of self-merit. God never yet gave to any person grace and everlasting life as a reward for merit. . . . The true way of salvation is this: First, a person must realize that he's a sinner, the kind of sinner who's congenitally unable to do any good thing. 'Whatsoever is not of faith is sin' (Rom. 14:23 KJV). Those who seek to earn the grace of God by their own efforts are trying to please God with sins. They mock God, and provoke His anger. The first step on the way to salvation is to repent."

—Martin Luther, *Commentary on the Epistle to the Galatians*

I want to believe
that there is another way.
I want to think
that I am the exception to the rule.
I grasp at the thought
that my righteousness is enough.
I hold to the hope
that my behavior satisfies you.
I want to think
that you judge me worthy.
It is my evaluation
that I am capable of your standard.
I want to hold on to my assessment
that I am not like others;
I can plainly see
that they offend your law.
I get the fact
that they fall short of your glory.
I know very well
that they can't stand before you.
But I still want to think
that I am not like them.
I want to hold your word
and my righteousness at the same
   time.
I want to celebrate the gospel
and my worthiness together.
But it is
a self-sufficient delusion.
It aggrandizes me and diminishes
   you.
It minimizes sin and devalues grace.
It asks the law to do
what only grace can accomplish.
It denies the daily evidence
of my sin.
It ignores the true condition
of my heart.
It turns away
from the sacrifice that you have made.
It omits the sovereign plan
of your grace.

It forgets the desperate condition
of my need.
And so I turn
to what I know is true.
I am nothing
without you.
I accept the invitation
of your grace.
I run to the sacrifice
of the cross.
I cry for the help
of your spirit.
I accept the diagnosis
of your word.
I trust the faithfulness
of your love.
I seek the forgiveness
you alone can give.
And I reject
the righteousness that is my own.

_____

God looks down from heaven
*   on the children of man*
to see if there are any who understand,
*   who seek after God.*
They have all fallen away;
*   together they have become corrupt;*
there is none who does good,
*   not even one. (Ps. 53:2–3)*

Why might it be difficult to fathom
God's grace as completely covering
all your fallenness?

Are you ever tempted to think that
you are less in need of God's saving
grace than others?

For further study and encouragement,
read Romans 3.

Psalm 47 (*Remix)*

Clap!
Clap!
Clap!
Wherever you are.
Whoever you are.
Shout!
Shout!
Shout!
Sing to God the song that
never ends.
Sing songs of joy,
songs of victory,
songs of redemption,
songs of sovereignty,
songs of majesty.
Your Savior is the Lord
Most High.
Your God is one to
be feared.
Your Redeemer is the
King of the earth.
He has chosen you to be the
object of his love.
He has called you to be the
focus of his grace.
Shout!
Shout!
Shout!
Clap!
Clap!
Clap!

Sing!
Sing!
Sing!
Your Savior reigns.
The nations belong to him.
The earth belongs to him.
Everything is owned by him.
Creation submits to him.
Rulers bow to him.
Praise!
Praise!
Praise!
Sing the song that
never ends.
Gather once again and exalt the
Exalted One.

———

Clap your hands, all peoples!
  Shout to God with loud songs of
    joy!
For the Lord, the Most High, is to be
    feared,
  a great king over all the earth.
    (Ps. 47:1–2)

How are you tempted to be passive in
your Christian life?

What events in your life make you
clap and shout? When you think
about the glory of God, how do you
respond?

For further study and encouragement,
read Revelation 19.

The Wisdom of Pain

The understanding
and appreciation of
wonderful things
often comes in the context of
the pain of
unwanted,
unplanned,
unexpected things.
Gratitude for
provided things
most powerfully comes
in the context of
want and need.
The joy of being
eternally loved
is most vibrant
in moments when you
feel unloved.

The recognition of
the value of wisdom
is most powerful
when you feel like a
fool.
You celebrate
divine strength the most
when
you've got no strength
of your own.
It really is true
that the lily
looks most beautiful,
not next to another
lily,
but next to a
rock.

Count it all joy, my brothers, when you meet trials of various kinds, for you know that the testing of your faith produces steadfastness. And let steadfastness have its full effect, that you may be perfect and complete, lacking in nothing. (James 1:2-4)

When suffering enters your life, how are you tempted to respond? Do you count it all joy?

In what situations in your life right now are you forgetting about God and his strength? When are you tempted to question his goodness and doubt his love?

For further study and encouragement, read 1 Peter 1.

Ready, Willing, and Waiting

Lord,
I think I can honestly say that
I am ready, willing, and waiting.
Ready, willing, and waiting
to see my sin as you see it.
Ready, willing, and waiting
to acknowledge that I am my biggest
    problem.
Ready, willing, and waiting
to run from wrong.
Ready, willing, and waiting
to seek your help.
Ready, willing, and waiting
for my mind to be clear.
Ready, willing, and waiting
for my heart to be clean.
Ready, willing, and waiting
to acknowledge what you see.
Ready, willing, and waiting
to rest in your compassion.
Ready, willing, and waiting
to hide in your unfailing love.
Ready, willing, and waiting
to be washed by you.
Ready, willing, and waiting
to admit that I acted against you.
Ready, willing, and waiting
to prove that you are right and just.
Ready, willing, and waiting
to confess that my problem is from
    birth.
Ready, willing, and waiting
to examine within.

Ready, willing, and waiting
to be whiter than snow.
Ready, willing, and waiting
to hear joy and gladness.
Ready, willing, and waiting
for brokenness to give way to joy.
Ready, willing, and waiting
to have a steadfast heart.
Ready, willing, and waiting
to celebrate your grace once more.
Ready, willing, and waiting
to teach others your ways.
Ready, willing, and waiting
to help them turn back to you.
Ready, willing, and waiting
to have you save me from me.
Ready, willing, and waiting
to sing songs of your righteousness.
Ready, willing, and waiting
to declare your praise.
Ready, willing, and waiting
to bring the sacrifice of a broken
    heart.
Ready, willing, and waiting
to see your people prosper.
Ready, willing, and waiting
to see you worshiped as is your due.
But, I am also
ready, willing, and waiting
to be protected by your love.
I am ready, willing, and waiting
to be held by your grace.

I am ready, willing, and waiting
to be hidden in your mercy.
I am ready, willing, and waiting
to be defended by your power.
Because I know
that I won't always be
ready, willing, and waiting.

———

*Stay dressed for action and keep your
lamps burning, and be like men who are
waiting for their master to come home
from the wedding feast, so that they
may open the door to him at once when
he comes and knocks. Blessed are those
servants whom the master finds awake
when he comes. Truly, I say to you, he will
dress himself for service and have them
recline at table, and he will come and
serve them. (Luke 12:35–37)*

Does your heart feel ready to serve God
where he has called you today? Where
do you feel less than willing to obey
God's word in your life?

How can you find patience and joy as
you wait upon the Lord?

For further study and encouragement,
read Isaiah 26.

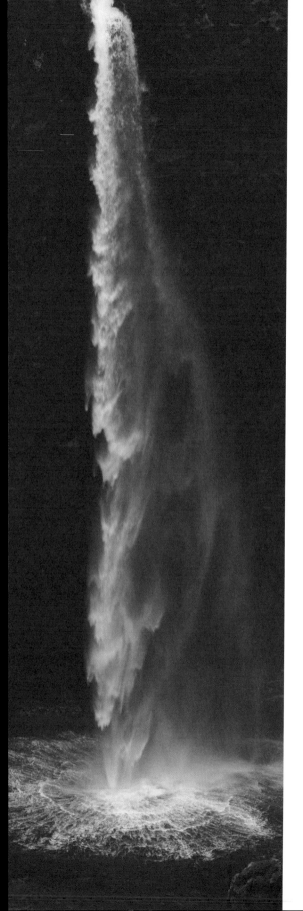

Days of Beauty

I have a vision problem.
My eyes are okay,
but my heart
doesn't see very well.
I live in a world
where your beauty
is everywhere visible.
It is there
in the lily.
It is there
in the cascading wave.
It is there
in the multihued sunset.
It is there
in the stars of the night.
It is there
in the power of the storm.
It is there
in the rhythm of the rain.
It is there
in the grandeur of the mountain.
It is there
in the lace of the clouds.
It is there
in the succulence of the apple.
It is there
everywhere I look.
But often
I do not see your beauty.
I must confess
I am so blind.
I see
my busy schedule.

I see
things to be fixed.
I see
obstacles to my plan.
I see
bills to be paid.
I see
things to be done.
I see,
but I fail to see your beauty.

Yet there is more:
I call things beautiful
that are not beautiful to you.
I am attracted to things
that you call ugly.
I even begin to believe
that there are things
more beautiful
than you.
And I want these things more
than you.
So I serve these things more
than you.
So, Lord,
correct my vision.
Please restore
the eyes of my heart.
Graciously make
the days that I have left
to be
days of beauty

because my heart
is filled
with visions of you.

———

But, as it is written,

> *"What no eye has seen, nor ear*
> *heard,*
> *nor the heart of man imagined,*
> *what God has prepared for those*
> *who love him"—*

these things God has revealed to us
through the Spirit. For the Spirit
searches everything, even the depths
of God. (1 Cor. 2:9–10)

In the ordinary moments of your
life, how often do you see the beauty
of God?

How often do you talk about God
with other people: your children,
your spouse, your friends? When you
share videos, books, photos, nature,
or links with others, do you point
their hearts to God?

For further study and encouragement,
read Psalm 119.

My Story

Unthinkable,
mysterious,
surprising,
amazing,
mind-bending,
blessed,
humbling.
How is it that this is
my life?
How is it that I have been
chosen?
How is it that I have been
accepted?
How is it that I have been
forgiven?
How is it that I have been
loved?
How is it that I have been
rescued?
How is it that I am now
called?
How is it that you would
take me,
mold me,
send me,
and use me?
Why would you care to redeem
my failures?
Why would you work to sanctify
my sufferings?
Why would you think to give me
gifts?

Why would you teach me your
gospel?
Why would you fill my mouth with
truth to say?
Why would you bless me with
the motivation to fight,
words to speak,
gifts to give,
service to offer,
and a reason to live?
Why would you comfort me in
my sorrows?
Why would you strengthen me in
my weaknesses?
Why would you forgive me for
my failures?
Why would you restore me when
I've wandered?
Compared to anything else
I have experienced or
known,
you are a
glorious mystery,
and your amazing grace is a
divine surprise.
It will be the theme of my
eternal song.
It will be the object of my
never-ending praise.
It will be the focus of my
study forever.
You are your grace.

The answer to all my questions is you.
My life is what it is because there is no one like you.

———

To [his saints] God chose to make known how great among the Genitles are the riches of the glory of this mystery, which is Christ in you, the hope of glory. (Col. 1:27)

What thoughts steal your meditations away from God? What often captures your mind, controls your thoughts, and dominates the desires of your heart?

How can you redirect your thoughts to the glorious mystery of God's grace?

For further study and encouragement, read Hebrews 2.

Surrender

It's not comfortable following you.
It's not predictable in your care.
It's not easy surrendering to your will.
It's not always ease that your grace gives.
Sometimes your grace gifts me with
hardship,
the unexpected travail,
the unplanned discipline,
the unwanted suffering,
the difficult trial,
the disappointing grief,
the disconcerting mystery,
and the uncomfortable.
Each is a tool—
an instrument of rescuing grace
never meant to harm,
never sent to condemn,
never intended to punish,
never a sign of your absence,
never a sign of your rejection—
and is always the right tool
to accomplish just what is needed
at just the right moment
in just the right way
to do just what is required
to rescue me from me,
to cause my heart to turn,
to help blind eyes to see,
to enable desires to transform,
to free me from my bondage to me,
and to enable me to truly love you
so that I would find joy
in daily,
heartfelt,
worshipful,
willing,
joyful
surrender to you.

———

Our Father in heaven,
hallowed be your name.
Your kingdom come,
your will be done,
on earth as it is in heaven.
Give us this day our daily bread,
and forgive us our debts,
as we also have forgiven our debtors.
And lead us not into temptation,
but deliver us from evil. (Matt. 6:9-13)

Read the Lord's Prayer above. When you pray, are you really asking for your own will, or God's will, to be done?

Do you find freedom, joy, and hope as you surrender to God in prayer?

For further study and encouragement, read Jonah 4 and Micah 6:8.

Watch Out for the Flesh Eaters!

I wish that it were
peacetime,
but
right now
you can't live that way.
Temptation is all around.
It's a smile,
a whisper,
a wish,
an invitation,
a sword.
There's little escape,
so little time to rest;
evil flirts with you
but will consume your flesh.
Do you really think
you're not at risk?
Has your enemy
lost his power
to tempt,
to seduce,
to ensnare,
to trap?

Do you really have
the liberty
to coast,
to rest,
to relax,
to slide on through?
When no day is an escape,
there's seldom rest;
evil hungers
to digest your flesh.
There is war being made;
darkness and light,
truth and lie,
right and wrong,
wise and foolish,
holy and sin,
God and the devil,
demon and friend.
So there's little escape.
There's precious little rest.
Evil lurks out there;
it will eat your flesh.

This world
is shattered glass.
It does not look,
it does not do
as designed.
You are infected
with the disease.
You are flawed
from within.
Sin still lives.
It is a law,
a war,
a prison,
a trap,
a drug.
Not many roads of escape,
not really much rest;
evil sings to you
but will devour your flesh.
There is but one
escape.
Just one thing
you can do.
Focus your eyes on
what you see.
Fix your gaze.
Look at the beauty,
the treasure,
the majesty,
the glory
of the Lord.
Run to the temple.

Be in awe.
Be enthralled.
Meditate.
And remember
what's holy,
what's eternal,
what's gorgeous,
what's true.
Bask in the beauty.
It will rescue you.
Because there's little escape,
there's a famine of rest;
evil waits for you
but will dine on your flesh.

May beauty be
your fortress.
May glory be
your rock.
May the Lord be
your refuge
until the war
is over,
until you've arrived
at rest,
until evil has been
crushed,
and you're home at last.
For now there's scant escape,
there's a real lack of rest;
evil hunts for you
to consume your flesh.

_____

*Humble yourselves, therefore, under
the mighty hand of God so that at the
proper time he may exalt you, casting
all your anxieties on him, because he
cares for you. Be sober-minded; be
watchful. Your adversary the devil
prowls around like a roaring lion,
seeking someone to devour. Resist
him, firm in your faith, knowing that
the same kinds of suffering are being
experienced by your brotherhood
throughout the world. And after you
have suffered a little while, the God
of all grace, who has called you to his
eternal glory in Christ, will himself
restore, confirm, strengthen, and
establish you. To him be the dominion
forever and ever. Amen. (1 Pet. 5:6–11)*

Every day, a war of kingdoms is
played out in your life. In your
struggle against sin, are you acting
like it's peacetime or wartime?

When the Holy Spirit convicts you of
sin, do you believe that it is condem-
nation or rescue? Do you run toward
conviction or away from it?

For further study and encouragement,
read Hebrews 4.

A Matter of the Heart

Remember Israel—
on the way to make
sacrifice
to Jehovah,
they stopped and did
homage
to Baal.
Remember Judas—
he attended the supper
after he
sold
Jesus for a little
silver.
Remember the Pharisees—
so publicly
committed,
yet they plotted Jesus's
death.
What seems
so very spiritual
on the surface
may not in reality
be a matter of
worship,
commitment,
integrity,
sacrifice,
and surrender
of the heart.

———

In sacrifice and offering you have not
delighted,
but you have given me an open ear.
Burnt offering and sin offering
you have not required. . . .
But may all who seek you
rejoice and be glad in you;
may those who love your salvation
say continually, "Great is the
Lord!" (Ps. 40:6, 16)

How do you measure your fruitfulness as a Christian? In what ways are you tempted to boast in your knowledge, skill, habits, or experience?

Read 1 Samuel 16:7. How are you blind to your true condition? How can you train your eyes to see what God sees?

For further study and encouragement, read Luke 18:9–14.

Sacrifices

Perhaps
if I give you
some of my time,
perhaps
if I give you
some of my strength,
perhaps
if I give you
some of my things,
perhaps
if I give you
some of my thoughts,
perhaps
if I give you
some of my success,
perhaps
if I give you
some of my relationships,
then
surely
these sacrifices
will bring you delight;
surely
these offerings
will bring you joy.
I'm quite willing
to give a tithe.
I'm quite willing
to interrupt
my schedule.
I'm quite willing
to volunteer
to serve.
I'm quite willing
to do
my part.
But I get the sense
that you're not satisfied
with a piece of me.
I get the sense
that the momentary giving,
momentary service,
momentary sacrifice,
momentary ministry,
momentary attention
of my heart to you
will not satisfy you.
But I'm afraid
of what you require.
I'm afraid of a
broken spirit.
I'm afraid of a
contrite heart.
I'm afraid to be
crushed by your grace.
So I try to
distract you
with my service,
distract you
with my time,
distract you
with my money.
Deep inside

I know what you want.
Deep inside
I know what you require.
I'm afraid
because I want to hold on to
my heart.
I want
to give it to other things.
I want to
pursue pleasures
outside of you.
I'm afraid
to give you
what would satisfy you.
I'm afraid of a
broken heart.
So I regularly offend you
with empty offerings
and vacuous praise.
And I hope
to my own destruction
that you'll be satisfied.

———

Offer right sacrifices,
  and put your trust in the LORD.
    (Ps. 4:5)

As humans, we are very good at
minimizing our sin. What patterns of
sin are you minimizing in your life?

How does minimizing your sin, and
not being broken over your sin,
devalue God's grace?

For further study and encouragement,
read 1 Peter 4:10-11.

Not Yours

I cannot say my heart is pure.
No—
not because it is riddled with lust
or
stained with hatred,
but because
it does not always long for you.
My heart longs
for comfort and ease,
for power and control,
for possessions and position,
for acceptance and recognition.
It longs for so many of the things
that carry the promise of
satisfaction,
contentment,
happiness,
and joy.
Yet, my heart is wired for you,
wired
to only rest in the rest found
in you.
It would be easy to reason
that I am okay.
I am not a thief.
I am not a murderer.
I have not stolen the spouse of
    another.
But this reality I cannot escape:
my heart is not pure,
because it does not always
long for you.
I have hated in my heart.

I have stolen with my thoughts.
I have lusted in secret.
I have done all these things
because my heart
doesn't always belong to you.
Lord, once more draw my heart to
    you.
Capture my thoughts.
Command my desires.
Submit my will.
Direct my plans.
Make my heart pure,
not because it is free of struggle,
but because
it no longer seeks
identity,
meaning,
peace,
purpose,
or that inner sense of well-being
outside of you.
When my heart finds life in you,
it will no longer
seek it in another.
I wish I could say I am pure,
but the battle still rages
and rescue is still needed
so that the longings of my heart
will not pull me away,
but will draw me
ever closer
to you.

———

The LORD saw that the wickedness of man was great in the earth, and that every intention of the thoughts of his heart was only evil continually. (Gen. 6:5)

How are you tempted to see yourself as a "good" person? Why is this a dangerous view?

See Romans 7:21–25. Where can you find rescue in your struggle against sin?

For further study and encouragement, read Matthew 5.

Grace Comes Down

Rebellion raises its ugly head
then grace comes down.
Darkness covers creation's light
then grace comes down.
Thorns and disease infect
then grace comes down.
People lie and cheat
then grace comes down.
Desires lead astray
then grace comes down.

Image bearers murder their own
then grace comes down.
Power corrupts the powerful
then grace comes down.
Pride's delusion ensnares
then grace comes down.
Fools preach what is foolish
then grace comes down.
Idols abound and deceive
then grace comes down.
The whole earth groans
then grace comes down.
Tears replace smiles
then grace comes down.
Hate hates love
then grace comes down.
Hope devolves to fear
then grace comes down.
Abuse victimizes care
then grace comes down.
Thievery robs generosity
then grace comes down.
Peace fights war
then grace comes down.
Danger lurks in every heart
then grace comes down.
Evil kidnaps minds
then grace comes down.
Morality lies shattered
then grace comes down.
Justice is unjust
then grace comes down.
Creatures are separated from their
    Creator
then grace comes down.

People cry, God weeps
then grace comes down
in the person,
in the birth,
of the Messiah child,
Jesus.

———

What then shall we say to these things? If God is for us, who can be against us? He who did not spare his own Son but gave him up for us all, how will he not also with him graciously give us all things? Who shall bring any charge against God's elect? It is God who justifies. (Rom. 8:31–33)

What price did God pay to redeem you?

If God paid such a price for your redemption, can you trust him for everything else that you need? What will this trust look like in your life today?

For further study and encouragement, read Ephesians 2.

Temptation

It is a new day,
but deep in my heart
I feel the unwanted tug
of temptation's draw.
I am tempted to permit my eyes
to focus on what they
should not see,
to permit my mind to contemplate
what it should not consider,
to let my hands grasp
what they should not hold,
to let my mouth speak words
it should never say,
to let my desires seek
what they should not crave,
to give my energies to
what is not your will,
to demand of others
what I should not require,
to let my feet walk
where they should not go,
to allow my ears to listen
to what they should never hear,
to treat my faculties
as if they belonged to me,
to approach my day
without reference to you,
and to put me and what I want
at the center once again.
Proving again
that my only hope in life
is that you offer me mercies
that are new every tempting morning.

––––––

Now the law came in to increase the trespass, but where sin increased, grace abounded all the more, so that, as sin reigned in death, grace also might reign through righteousness leading to eternal life through Jesus Christ our Lord. (Rom. 5:20–21)

Where are you struggling against temptation today?

Read Mark 7:14–23. Do your temptations start with the sin inside you or outside you? Then read Hebrews 4:16. How does the ministry of the Holy Spirit offer help in your time of need?

For further study and encouragement, read Romans 8.

Your Law

I have come to understand
that if I fail to love
your law,
I will fail to esteem
your grace.
If I fail to respect
your judgment,
I will fail to celebrate
your mercy.
I have come to acknowledge
that if I fail to fear
your anger,
I will fail to seek
your forgiveness.
If I fail to admit
my idolatry,
I will fail to cry out for
your rescue.
I have come to grasp
that it is only when I accept
the worst news ever to be
written,
that I will then gladly hear
the best news ever to be
proclaimed.
It is only when I give up
hope in me,
that I will put my
hope in you.
It is only when I abandon
my righteousness,
that I will rest in
your righteousness.
So, I pray that you would grant me
the grace
to see and accept the indictment of
your law,
so I will seek and celebrate
your grace.

I rejoice at your word
 like one who finds great spoil.
I hate and abhor falsehood,
 but I love your law.
Seven times a day I praise you
 for your righteous rules.
Great peace have those who love your
  law;
 nothing can make them stumble.
I hope for your salvation, O LORD,
 and I do your commandments.
My soul keeps your testimonies;
 I love them exceedingly.
I keep your precepts and testimonies,
 for all my ways are before you.
Let my cry come before you, O LORD;
 give me understanding according
  to your word!
Let my plea come before you;
 deliver me according to your word.
My lips will pour forth praise,
 for you teach me your statutes.
My tongue will sing of your word,
 for all your commandments are
  right.

Let your hand be ready to help me,
 for I have chosen your precepts.
I long for your salvation, O LORD,
 and your law is my delight.
Let my soul live and praise you,
 and let your rules help me.
I have gone astray like a lost sheep;
 seek your servant,
 for I do not forget your command-
  ments. (Ps. 119:162–176)

When you sin, what or whom do you blame? Is your problem due to your environment or your heart?

See Psalm 16. How does God show you that the boundaries of his law are good?

For further study and encouragement, read Romans 5.

Sleep

Go to sleep.
You are there with me
every resting moment.
Watched by your faithful eye,
dreams come and go,
but you are still there with me
through the night.
Sun shines, day comes,
and I am not alone—
greeted by your presence,
held by your care,
your mercies once again brand-new
for what I don't yet know
but will have to face.
Day comes in on me,
situations and locations;
you go where you ask me to go,
and you enable me to do what you ask
    me to do.
Temptations come, and you are
my defense.
Discouragements come, and you are
my encouragement.
Night falls, but I am not afraid
and not troubled by regret,
for you protect me
and your forgiveness covers my sin.
When my last breath comes,
you will be with me,
and, as the years of eternity span,
you will still be with me
forever.

_____

There are many who say, "Who will
    show us some good?
    Lift up the light of your face upon
    us, O Lᴏʀᴅ!"
You have put more joy in my heart
    than they have when their grain
    and wine abound.
In peace I will both lie down and sleep;
    for you alone, O Lᴏʀᴅ, make me
    dwell in safety. (Ps. 4:6-8)

What keeps you up at night?

Do your circumstances change your
joy and peace? How?

For further study and encouragement,
read about the God who never
changes in Numbers 23:19; Malachi
3:6; Hebrews 13:8; and James 1:17.

You're Not

When I'm
weary and exhausted,
you're not.
When I'm
confused and discouraged,
you're not.
When I'm
fickle and unfaithful,
you're not.
When I'm
doubtful and disheartened,
you're not.
When I'm
fearful and anxious,
you're not.
When I'm
short-sighted and fearful,
you're not.
When I'm
tired and about to quit,
you're not.
When I'm
lacking in hope and love,
you're not.
When I'm
shocked and surprised,
you're not.
When I'm
angrily withholding grace,
you're not.
When I'm
unfaithful to what I've promised,
you're not.

When I'm
selfish and disloyal,
you're not.
Oh, Lord of
faithfulness and grace,
I am so thankful
that
in those moments
when I'm
losing my way,
you're not.

———

Now may the God of peace himself
sanctify you completely, and may
your whole spirit and soul and body
be kept blameless at the coming of our
Lord Jesus Christ. He who calls you is
faithful; he will surely do it.
(1 Thess. 5:23–24)

When you are anxious or weary, are
you afraid that others will see your
weakness and think less of you? Are
you afraid that God will see your
weakness and be disappointed in you?

Read 2 Timothy 2:13. Does our security
depend on our own faithfulness?

For further study and encouragement,
read Isaiah 40.

This One

The little one who was born
outside the circles of
power
would someday die
outside the city walls.
That child not recognized
in halls of
wisdom
was wisdom come to earth.
The little one who would soon
flee for his life
came to be the giver of
life.
This one who would know
so much rejection
would purchase
acceptance
for all who believe.
This one who would know
hunger
came as the bread to
satisfy hungry hearts.
This little one born with
no home
came to secure our heavenly home.
This one who would have
no throne
came to establish his throne
in the hearts of his own.
This one who would be
forsaken by his own
came so we would never be forsaken.
All that we would not want
to face,
all that we would not want
to endure,
all that we would not want
to suffer,
he faced,
he endured,
and he suffered
righteously,
willingly,
and lovingly
for this one thing—
our salvation.

———

Jesus said to them, "I am the bread of life; whoever comes to me shall not hunger, and whoever believes in me shall never thirst. But I said to you that you have seen me and yet do not believe. All that the Father gives me will come to me, and whoever comes to me I will never cast out. For I have come down from heaven, not to do my own will but the will of him who sent me. And this is the will of him who sent me, that I should lose nothing of all that he has given me, but raise it up on the last day. For this is the will of my Father, that everyone who looks on the Son and believes in him should have eternal life, and I will raise him up on the last day." (John 6:35-40)

Has your heart become too familiar with the miracle of the incarnation? Do you only think about the gift of Jesus at Christmas?

How can you reflect this week on the saving blood of Jesus? With whom can you share this eternal good news?

For further study and encouragement, read Psalm 22.

Why Bother?

I consider
the brokenness of the world,
and I think,
"Why bother?"

I look
at the corruption all around me,
and I cry,
"Why bother?"

I wonder at
my inability to live with my neighbor,
and I ask,
"Why bother?"

I face
my war with sin inside and outside,
and I ponder,
"Why bother?"

I look
at the problems of the culture around
    me,
and I lament,
"Why bother?"

I scan
my world broken by disease and
    misuse,
and in sadness I say,
"Why bother?"

I consider
the statistics of violence and abuse,
and I think,
"Why bother?"

I am assaulted
with the reality of endless wars
        between nations,
and overwhelmed I say,
"Why bother?"

I am defeated
by temptation's power,
and I cry,
"Why bother?"

I ponder
how good is called bad and bad good,
and my frustration says,
"Why bother?"

I search
for hope like a parched man for water,
but end up thinking,
"Why bother?"

I look
to myself and see weakness and want,
and my grief says,
"Why bother?"

Perhaps
I should live for leisure and comfort
and give into,
"Why bother?"

Maybe
I should exist for the here and now,
and forgetting forever, say,
"Why bother?"

I am tempted
to live for power and control
and of greater things say,
"Why bother?"

Perhaps
personal pleasure in the here and now
is what it's all about, so
"Why bother?"

But in
exhaustion I look up and not around,
and I say,
"Why bother?"
Because you are, and you are good.
"Why bother?"
Because you dispense goodness and
    grace.
"Why bother?"
Because you bring life out of death.
"Why bother?"
Because you have a plan, and it will
    be done.
"Why bother?"
Because I have been welcomed into
    your kingdom of life.
"Why bother?"
Because I am always with you.
It is true
that my eyes don't always see
and my heart isn't always confident.
It is true that darkness overwhelms me
and fear leaves me weak.

But you come near.
You remind me once again
that I can be confident
because
you were unwilling to say,
"Why bother?"

————

*"Be strong and courageous. Do not
be afraid or dismayed before the king
of Assyria and all the horde that is
with him, for there are more with us
than with him. With him is an arm of
flesh, but with us is the Lord our God,
to help us and to fight our battles."
And the people took confidence from
the words of Hezekiah king of Judah.
(2 Chron. 32:7–8)*

Are you tempted to be depressed
about your circumstances?

Read Hebrews 4:14–16. What specific
truths about Jesus transform your
mind and renew your faith?

For further study and encouragement,
read Isaiah 51.

Dissatisfied

Your dissatisfaction
is my hope.
Your discontent
is my redemption.
Your unwillingness
to stop,
to quit,
to give up and walk away,
to turn your back on what you've
    begun,
to grow weary,
to become impatient,
to turn from grace to judgment,
is my salvation.
Every day I arise to hope
with reason to continue,
with motivation to press on,
with energy for the battle,
because I know
you will not relent,
you will not quit,
you will not be satisfied or content,
until every microbe of sin
has been removed
from every cell
of every heart
of every one of your children.
Then and only then
will you declare victory
and invite your children
into the kingdom
you have prepared for them.

But when [Jesus] heard it, he said, "Those who are well have no need of a physician, but those who are sick. Go and learn what this means: 'I desire mercy, and not sacrifice.' For I came not to call the righteous, but sinners." (Matt. 9:12-13)

Are you satisfied with yourself and your Christian walk? When you are content and satisfied with yourself, how much grace do you need?

Do you have other people in your life whom God uses to help you see your sin? Are you humble and approachable when they bring observations to you?

For further study and encouragement, read Hebrews 12.

You Came!

You came!
You came!
You came!
It's unbelievable,
unimaginable.
It's beautiful.
In love different than ever seen,
you left glory
to display glory
to those who had forsaken glory
for earthly things.
You came!
You came!
You came!
Willing to leave splendor,
willing to come to a broken place,
willing to suffer,
willing to be rejected,
willing to face injustice,
willing to die.
You came!
You came!
You came!
Not because we deserved you,
not because we earned your presence,
not because of our achievements,
not because we were worthy of your
    love.
You came!
You came!
You came!

Moved by your glory,
propelled by your love,
sent by your grace,
driven to redeem,
you came!

———

*For while we were still weak, at
the right time Christ died for the
ungodly. For one will scarcely die for a
righteous person—though perhaps for
a good person one would dare even to
die—but God shows his love for us in
that while we were still sinners, Christ
died for us. (Rom. 5:6-8)*

Has the gospel become too familiar
in your heart? Are you no longer
amazed at the grace that came down
to sinners?

What specific truths about Jesus will
renew your awe in the gospel?

For further study and encouragement,
read Colossians 1.

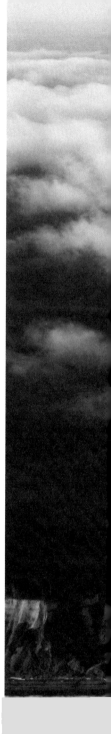

Death of Death

Death
is all around me.
People kill people.
Death
is all around me.
Disease kills people.
Death
is all around me.
Accidents kill people.
Death
is all around me.
Machines kill people.
Death
is all around me.
Storms kill people.
Death
is all around me.
Every living thing
is in the process of dying.
Death
is all around me.
But in death's
night,
in the gloom of the
grave,
as the sad drone of
mourning
seems to shatter
hope,
I see a light.
I hear your
voice.
You remind me once again that
death
will one day be forever
behind me.
For on the
cross
and out from the
grave,
you conquered death
and you guaranteed that
death
will finally and forever
die.

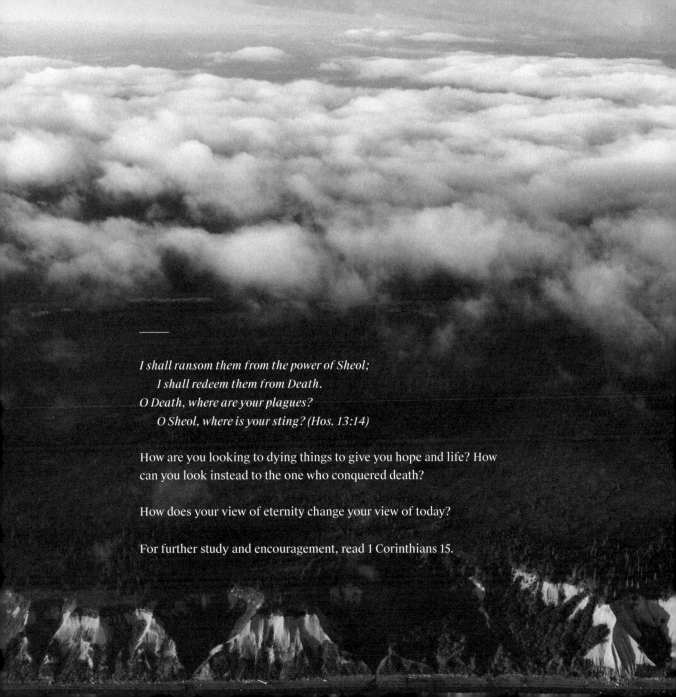

———

I shall ransom them from the power of Sheol;
  I shall redeem them from Death.
O Death, where are your plagues?
  O Sheol, where is your sting? (Hos. 13:14)

How are you looking to dying things to give you hope and life? How can you look instead to the one who conquered death?

How does your view of eternity change your view of today?

For further study and encouragement, read 1 Corinthians 15.

What You Want

It is often and sadly
true
that what I want
for me
and what you want
for me
do not agree.
My mind tells me
that what you want
for me
is gloriously better,
that you are
wise,
loving,
patient,
sovereign,
holy,
good,
that all of your ways are
right and true,
that you would never lead me into
temptation,
and that you always deliver me from
evil.
But here is my
problem.
There are wandering ways in my
heart.

The eyes of my heart don't always
focus on what is
beautiful,
wholesome,
good,
right,
and true
in your eyes,
so again I pray
for the rescue that only comes from
you—
not rescue from the things around me
that capture my gaze,
that kidnap my desires,
that lure me away.
No,
I need to be protected from
me,
I need to be rescued from what I
want,
so that what you want for
me;
will win yet another
battle
in my heart.

———

The Lᴏʀᴅ is righteous in all his ways
*   and kind in all his works.*
The Lᴏʀᴅ is near to all who call on him,
*   to all who call on him in truth. (Ps. 145:17–18)*

What regularly kidnaps your desires away from God?

When your heart wanders from God, are you quicker to hide your sin or confess it?

For further study and encouragement, read Psalm 121.

Wait

I have come to
understand
that I am not the
author
of my own story.
My narrative
is being penned
by one
who is the definition
of all that is
wise,
loving,
pure,
true,
and good.
But since I am
in the story but not the
author of the story,

I am often called
to wait.
I wish I could say
that I wait well,
but I don't.
I wish I could say
that I never question
your wisdom,
but I do.
So, Lord,
once more I ask for the
grace to wait,
not only so I can get
what I'm waiting for,
but so that I will become
what you want me to become
as I wait.

_____

*I wait for the L*ORD*, my soul waits,*
    and in his word I hope;
my soul waits for the Lord
    more than watchmen for the morning,
    more than watchmen for the morning. (Ps. 130:5–6)

When you can't change your circumstances, do you get anxious? When you can't understand what God is doing, is it hard for you to wait on him?

How can you surrender to God's sovereignty as you wait? What spiritual disciplines can guide and encourage you during seasons of waiting?

For further study and encouragement, read Romans 4:18–21.

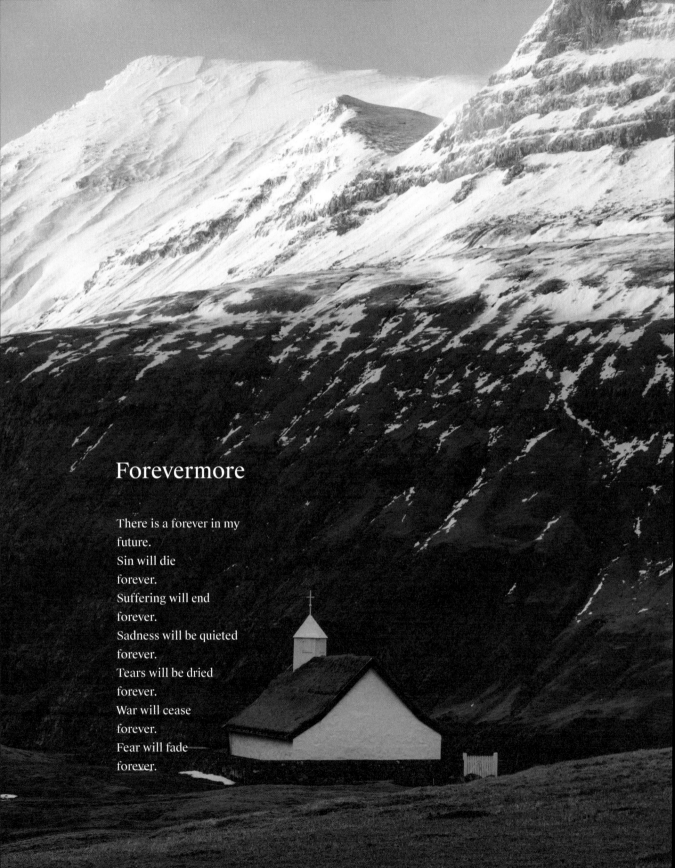

Forevermore

There is a forever in my
future.
Sin will die
forever.
Suffering will end
forever.
Sadness will be quieted
forever.
Tears will be dried
forever.
War will cease
forever.
Fear will fade
forever.

Satan will be defeated
forever.
Sickness will end
forever.
Hope will live
forever.
Grace will reign
forever.
Love will rule
forever.
Peace will prosper
forever.
Life will live
forever.
But, best of all,
glorious beyond imagination—
this I will not take for
granted,
I will live with it in
view,
I will not give in or
give up,
it will make my rocky journey
worth it—
your work in me and for me
will come to
completion,
and I will finally be
like you and
near you and
I will reign with you
forevermore!

———

*And I am sure of this, that he who
began a good work in you will bring
it to completion at the day of Jesus
Christ. (Phil. 1:6)*

In the intense moments of your day,
when you are tempted to express
sinful anger, what kingdom does it
look like you're hoping for—your
own little kingdom, or God's forever
kingdom?

Where do you look for hope?

For further study and encouragement,
read Revelation 7.

Previously Published Poems

"Awake Again," "Broken-Down House," "Celebration," "Eavesdrop on Eternity," "Good and Angry," "The Good Life," "Identity Amnesia," "Legacy," "A Light in His Hands," "A Matter of the Heart," "Me and Mine," "My Calling," "Revelation," "Secret Wish," "Wait," and "You Are Not Like Me" were published in Paul David Tripp, *Broken Down House* (Shepherd Press, 2009). Reproduced in this volume with permission.

"The Dance of Redemption," "God's Pleasure," "The Holy of Holies," "Hoping for a Broken Heart," "Moral Vulnerability," "Nathan's Legacy," "No More 'If Only'," "Not Like David?" "Ready, Willing, and Waiting," "Romans 7," "Sacrifices," "Somebody Else," "Something in My Hands I Bring," "Unfailing Love," and "When God Is Glad" were published in Paul David Tripp, *Whiter Than Snow* (Wheaton, IL: Crossway, 2008).

"Days of Beauty," "Family Forever," "Fearless Forever," "Functional Blindness," "Goodness," "Hearts at Rest," "Mercy Prayer," "Not Yours," "One Thing," "The Rejection of Rejection," "Rest," "Safe," "Sign Beauty," "The Theology of Beauty," "Two Words You Never Want to Hear," "Uber Music," "Under Attack," "Watch Out for the Flesh Eaters," "Why Bother?," "Why I Hate to Wait," and "The Worship of Another" were published in Paul David Tripp, *A Shelter in the Time of Storm* (Wheaton, IL: Crossway, 2009).

About the Photographer

Tim Kellner is a photographer and filmmaker based in New York. The photography included in this book contains images from all around the world that were taken over five years. For the project, Kellner traveled to ten countries and five continents. The photograpy selections are meant to reflect the content and themes contained within the poetry. You can find more of Kellner's work on Instagram and YouTube.

Photo Index

Scripture Index